Do-It-Yourself Early Learning

DO-IT-YOURSELF
EARLY LEARNING

EASY AND FUN ACTIVITIES AND TOYS FROM EVERYDAY HOME CENTER MATERIALS

JEFF A. JOHNSON & TASHA A. JOHNSON

Redleaf Press®
www.redleafpress.org
800-423-8309

Published by Redleaf Press
10 Yorkton Court
St. Paul, MN 55117
www.redleafpress.org

First edition 2006
Cover designed by Percolator
Cover photos by Jeff Johnson
Interior typeset in Whitney and designed by Percolator
Interior photos by Jeff, Tasha, and Zoë Johnson
Printed in the United States of America

Library of Congress Cataloging-in-Publication Data

Johnson, Jeff A., 1969–
    Do-it-yourself early learning : easy and fun activities and toys from everyday home center materials / Jeff A. Johnson and Tasha A. Johnson.
       p. cm.
    ISBN 978-1-929610-81-5
    1. Play. 2. Early childhood education. 3. Child care. 4. Educational toys. 5. Toy making.   I. Johnson, Tasha, 1969- II. Title.
    HQ782.J634 2005
    649'.55—dc22   2005028689

Printed on acid-free paper   U15-07

Dedicated to
Gordon Lee Johnson
Husband, Father, and Grandfather
6-04-47 to 2-17-02

He knew all there was to know about every
thingamajig, doohickey, and gizmo at the lumberyard
and always had time to explain them.

CONTENTS

ACKNOWLEDGMENTS

We would like to thank all the providers who have helped us refine these projects during visits to their programs or during training sessions. Your contributions have helped make the content of this book stronger. We would like to offer special thanks to the following providers and programs for allowing us to interrupt their day to visit, play, and take pictures. You will never completely understand how important your contribution was to the creation of this book. Thank you for sharing your time, suggestions, and insights.

- Native American Child Care Center; Beach Husk and Tammy Sanford
- Country Living Child Care; Shanna Barton
- Mary Elizabeth Child Care Center; Jane Heider and Tammie Farrer
- Small World Child Care; Leslie Davis
- ABC Child Care; Erika McWell

We would also like to thank all the children who took every activity in this book out for "test drives" when we visited programs. Watching you play provided all kinds of new ideas and insights. Special thanks to Hunter, Maddie, Ty, Sam, Jack, RJ, Katie, Libby, and Simon for all the playing you did in our home and to our daughter, Zoë, for her many ideas and contributions.

We would love to hear from you. Please send your feedback to us at diyearlylearning@cableone.net.

INTRODUCTION

Much of my desire to build, tinker, and explore with many of the items used in this book came from childhood time spent with three important individuals. It has taken me over thirty years to recognize how truly important their contributions were in making me ME.

My father, Gordon Johnson, could fix or build almost anything. My fondest memory of him is riding home from the lumberyard on so many Saturday mornings, sharing a glass bottle of Coke and listening to talk radio. There is not enough room in this book to share all the things he helped me learn and discover.

As a child I spent as many hours as possible observing my grandfather, Oliver Olson, as he farmed the same small piece of North Dakota that his father farmed. He grew up outside, fixing, fiddling, and making do. One of the many things I learned from him was how to observe. He pointed out exciting things (baby foxes, emerging crops, geese, remains of 100-year-old sod houses) in what my city frame of mind thought was a bleak, empty landscape. He taught me to see in a different way, to look closely and carefully at things and situations.

I met Bill Reding when I was a preschooler and he was remodeling the house next door. I was curious about all the banging and business going on and he put me to work. He quickly became a family friend and taught me how to straighten bent nails, work hard, and take care of my tools. He treated me like a capable, competent, intelligent person, not a silly little kid. He gave me confidence and he shared his coffee and Trident chewing gum when it was break time.

One of the inherent negatives of working with young children is that you do not get to see the payoff—the final result of your hours of care and concern—for many, many years, if at all. In addition, the children may not realize how much you affected their lives until it is too late to acknowledge your contribution. In part, this book is a "thank you" to those three men who nurtured my boyhood curiosity and love of tools; they contributed to this book decades ago without knowing it would ever be written.

Play and Learning

"Parents and teachers often say that children who have discovered how to play in their preschool days transform their love of play into eagerness to learn when they go up to school." (Haller 1991, 92)

A major part of our job as providers of early care and education is to encourage that eagerness to learn in the children we serve. We keep them safe and healthy, we feed them nutritious meals, we love and nurture them, we allow them to try and then succeed or fail, we encourage exploration and discovery—all so they can head off to school primed and ready to continue learning. Our job is to help build children who will love learning not only while in school but throughout their entire lives. We help them develop the skills they need for school and then set them on their way; we build the foundation.

It is our hope that the activities in this book help you build a strong foundation for learning with the children in your care, but we do not want your efforts to construct do-it-yourself learning toys to stop here. It is our wish that you continue to look for simple, affordable, child-directed activities without all the superfluities of most store-bought toys. We also hope we have instilled in you the children's desire to play, explore, and discover. Here are three suggestions to help you journey down that road, once this book is dog-eared and your shelves are full of these learning materials:

- Expand on these ideas
- Keep tinkering
- Watch the children for more innovations

Expand on These Ideas

Look at the activities in this book as a starting point for your own projects. Expand on the ideas we have shared and make them your own. You have a wholly different set of experiences that brings a unique perspective to each activity. Use this experience to think up fresh variations for the projects we have shared. It is important to look for ways to meet the individual developmental needs of the children in your care. While most of these activities and variations will work for the majority of children, we have to keep in mind that alterations will be necessary for some children. Keep your eyes open for those special needs and ways to meet them.

Keep Tinkering

Even if you try out only a small number of the activities in this book, you probably already know your way around your favorite home center pretty well.

Use that knowledge to try new things. Wander around the home center, or any other place, look for interesting materials, and tinker with them. Explore new materials as the children in your care explore the activities in this book. Take some time and play with new objects, ideas, and concepts.

Try to replicate the curiosity and sense of wonder that children possess. See things through young eyes and look for fresh perspectives. Rejuvenate your curriculum with simple, uncomplicated, and undemanding activities that are child centered and developmentally appropriate.

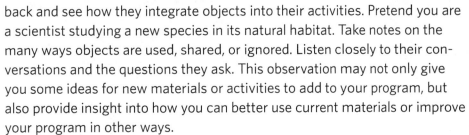

Watch the Children for More Innovations

We found that watching the children in our care is one of the best ways to come up with these fresh ideas. Sadly, providers often find themselves so busy taking care of everyone that they do not have time to observe. Make the time. Observe children at play; take the time to step back and see how they integrate objects into their activities. Pretend you are a scientist studying a new species in its natural habitat. Take notes on the many ways objects are used, shared, or ignored. Listen closely to their conversations and the questions they ask. This observation may not only give you some ideas for new materials or activities to add to your program, but also provide insight into how you can better use current materials or improve your program in other ways.

The most important thing to remember is that you are setting the stage for play. You are creating an environment where children are comfortable enough to take learning risks, where they have the time they need to fully explore materials, where it is okay to take risks and even make mistakes, and where play is an integral part of every day. Keep playing, keep exploring, keep discovering, and keep learning.

It's All About Relationships

If we look closely while children play, explore, and discover, we can actually see them learn and know we helped make that experience possible. The projects that follow are designed to help children become confident, stretch their intellect, and learn to explore and discover while they play. These are simple projects made with simple materials. To make them successful, the most important thing to remember is that in the end the children will recall the relationship with the caregiver more strongly than any individual project. Learning in early childhood is primarily about interpersonal contact. Years from now, children will recall the bits and pieces of *you* that enter their memories. The trust, the unconditional positive regard, the hugs, the shared soda and chewing gum are more important than the toys and projects. It *is* all about relationships.

Make sure they remember you well. Make them remember you as someone who thought they were worthy of time, someone who knew they were capable, intelligent, able, and competent. It is not an easy task, but it is an extraordinary gift to give a child. Tasha just reminded me that too many children grow up without an adult in their life who allows them to seek challenges, make mistakes, and learn through play, exploration, and discovery as the men I mentioned above did for me. I hope you try to be that person—to give that gift—to as many children as possible.

References

Haller, Ingeborg. 1991. *How children play.* Edinburgh, UK: Floris Books.

1

WHY MAKE YOUR OWN LEARNING TOYS?

> They [babies] arrive expecting to be cared for and protected. They are also born to learn, and their ability to learn—to make adaptive changes in their behavior on the basis of experience—is at its peak in the early years of life, when they are making the brain connections on which learning and living depend. —Ann Barnet and Richard Barnet, *The Youngest Minds*

Learning through play is as natural, important, and easy for young children as breathing. Both abilities are innate, programmed into their brains from the beginning. Healthy children are born wired and ready to breathe and they are born wired and ready to play. They have a natural curiosity, a desire to touch, taste, test, and traverse the world around them. They are programmed to test limits, make mistakes, and learn. Humankind's desire to explore new places and think new thoughts begins in infancy and is renewed with the birth of each successive generation.

This book will explain the construction and use of a variety of affordable, durable, engaging, and kid-tested play props, equipment, and activities designed to meet this innate need to play. The following projects are all built with materials readily available at your local home center. The most important component of each project is you, the care provider.

Early care and education professionals understand the importance of safe, child-centered, developmentally appropriate play in the lives of young children better today than ever before. We know that play is the tool children use to explore their environments, learn new skills, internalize new concepts, and make sense of the adult world during the whirlwind of brain development that takes place before the age of five.

We also understand that a vital part of our job involves setting the stage for such play. We provide children with the warm, safe, nurturing environment they need to take learning risks, invent, explore, and play. A child must have a strong relationship with her caregiver if she is to open up, take learning risks, and explore new materials, situations, and environments. As early childhood educators, we must set the stage for play. We must provide ample time for exploration of materials, practice, and repetition. This means operating in kids' time: unhurried, relaxed, and child directed.

The children we work with also need us to know when to introduce more complexity into an activity or play scenario. They need us to see when they are ready to move deeper, learn more, or expand their world and to know how to help them accomplish that next step. We have to be observant and take the lead from the children in our care.

Toys, Play, and Learning

The cartoonish color and visual noise will knock you off your feet when you walk into the local mall's toy store. Television and movie characters jump off the shelves as action figures, video games, and anything else upon which an image is printable. Toys, meant to be the tools children use in the work of play, have morphed into commercials for other products. They have lost much of their flexibility and killed creativity. It is sad to see a child chastised by peers when the play "script" is deviated from. "You can't do that! You're not playing right." The media hype and marketing tie-ins of too many toys leave children thinking that there is only one "right" way to play. They engage children momentarily and then are tossed aside for the next marketing gimmick.

Other products, marketed as "learning toys," overstimulate children with their electronic laughing, singing, flashing, banging, twisting, twirling, shaking, talking, rocking, and rolling. This overstimulation makes it difficult for children to focus and engage during other activities. They are so used to the hype provided by these obnoxious toys that they come to crave the flashing lights, annoying songs, and constant over-the-top stimulation they provide.

We are not proposing that you take to the streets and smash these overly commercial, overly mechanized, and overly stimulating toys as the Luddites destroyed factory machinery during the early years of the Industrial

Revolution, but we are proposing you spend your early learning material budget differently. We have found that the simple homemade learning projects and materials outlined in this book meet the needs of young children better than most of their ready-made counterparts.

Picture a young child, a cardboard box, and an hour of adult-free time. Play and creativity just happen. How many times have you seen a child open a present, look it over, and toss it aside to play with the packaging? Empty cardboard boxes, ranging in size from Froot Loops to refrigerator, open a world of exploration, open-ended play, and fun. When kids play on their own terms, they gravitate toward simple, flexible, generic materials.

Zoë, our daughter, spent her fifth birthday riding across South Dakota playing with a family of toothpicks. They were broken to different lengths to make a daddy, mommy, big brother, and sister . . . a toothpick-sized version of her own family. Her mind spun adventurous tales and mundane domestic stories as we rolled down the interstate.

The primary reason you should consider making your own learning toys is that they will stimulate children but not overstimulate them; they will engage children but not try to sell them anything during that engagement. These are simple, child-centered learning toys without the Madison Avenue hype, glitz, and packaging. The projects in this book will help you create simple playthings, with simple materials, that will engage imagination and creativity instead of smothering it with overhyped, overpriced, overly complicated store-bought toys. Here are some other reasons to make your own learning toys:

- They are affordable.
- They are durable.
- They are flexible.
- The materials are readily available.
- It's fun!

Affordability

We have never met a center director, preschool teacher, family child care provider, or early elementary teacher with too much money to spend on his or her program. Most early education programs do not have the financial support they need, and learning materials are often behind utilities, food, staff, and insurance on the funding priority list.

When providers do have funds to spend on equipment and supplies, they usually find high prices for quality merchandise. We made a concerted effort to keep the items described in this book affordable for caregivers. We wanted to offer an alternative to the high-priced items found in many stores and catalogs. Keeping things simple also kept them affordable.

Durability

We have tried to balance affordability and durability; with proper care, many of the items in this book will last the life of your program. Other things are inexpensive and will have shorter lives in your program. We tested all the projects, props, and activities in this book with actual children in real early learning environments, and they have stood up to the use and abuse those children dished out. One of our goals was to make sure you get your money's worth when you invest time and effort into making these projects.

Flexibility

Another great reason to make your own learning toys is the flexibility you have to make things just the way you want them. These projects are not set in stone. There is not one right way to make any of them. We have explored, experimented, and shared what worked best for us. You may see a whole new way to use the materials or projects we describe. Great. Try it your way. We hope these items will inspire creativity both in children and in adults.

Besides flexibility in construction, these projects also offer many possibilities for use. Each project description has a Variations section because they all can be used in many different ways, and we are sure you will think of many more. Use your imagination and learn from what you see while the kids are playing. Make changes and adjustments based on the needs of the children with whom you work.

Availability

One of the best reasons for making your own learning toys is that the needed materials are almost universally available. We cannot compete with the omnipresent cardboard box, but it is pretty easy to put your hands on the things you need to make all the projects in this book. We used easy-to-acquire materials and, when possible, we used the same materials in more than one project. The vast majority of the items you need to make these projects can be purchased at your favorite local home center. We did not want you to have to drive to five specialty stores to make one project. Take the book to the home center with you, point to an activity's material list while saying "I need this" to an employee, and she should be able to show you exactly what you need.

It's Fun

Making your own learning toys is fun. It is exciting to see children respond to materials that are new to them. Seeing them think as they explore and discover is a fascinating and invigorating experience. Watch their faces as they examine something new; you can almost see them thinking as they touch, turn, and take in the object. It is a very energizing and fun experience.

Involving the children in the creation of these projects is also fun. You will get a lot of joy from involving them in the construction process. The newness of the materials and activities, the children's wonderful questions and comments, as well as their desire to help, all come together to make the experience fun and rewarding.

2

WHAT KIDS LEARN
WHILE PLAYING

> *Young children do not differentiate between play, learning, and work.*
> —Cosby S. Rogers and Janet K. Sawyers, *Play in the Lives of Children*

Young children don't differentiate between play, learning, and work, and they do not plan or categorize their learning before, after, or while it is taking place. We have never met a preschooler who sits down at the breakfast table and says to the child next to him, "Hey, Maya, what's on your agenda today? I've got a full schedule; I plan to work on my small-muscle skills and then maybe spend some time on visual discrimination before snack. Then I'm going to focus on my toilet training and language skills until lunch. After that I'll be working on developing my interpersonal relationships." Children play, learn, work, explore, discover, research, experiment, and goof around all at the same time. They are constantly engaging their environments; wringing out as much learning as they can from their surroundings.

Their method of learning is holistic; they engage their mind, body, and spirit in all their learning so that the sum of what they learn is more than the individual parts. One activity, project, or toy can engage a child in a variety of different ways all at the same time. Singing a song while hopping, on one foot, from one paving stone to the next on a warm spring morning is a simple activity. The child, however, is learning a lot. She is gaining experiential knowledge about gravity, developing large- and small-muscle groups, honing her balance, getting to know what the warmth of the sun and coolness of the breeze on her skin feels like, improving her memory as she searches it for the words to the song, working on pronunciation and diction as she sings, bettering her depth perception, and many other things all at once. Most people see a child hopping and singing; they should see a scientist at work rediscovering the world.

Although the children do not categorize, plan, or label their learning, we adults can better understand what they are up to and help build the right environments for promoting early learning if we take the time to see what is happening when children play.

"Pipes, please!" two-year-old Hunter shouts as soon as he is in the house and notices that the clear plastic tote isn't on the floor in the center of the playroom where he left it the previous day. He takes Tasha's hand, leads her to the closet door and repeats, "Pipes, please!" It is quarter to eight in the morning and his mind is already racing. He is ready to work, to learn, and to play.

If you give a young child a tote full of PVC pipe lengths and fittings (or almost anything else), play simply happens. Their innate curiosity will draw them to the materials, and their visceral need to touch, explore, discover, and experiment will take over. They are on a journey to rediscover the world. Our job, as early educators, is to set the stage for this play, exploration, and rediscovery. Learning will happen without us, but by understanding more

about the learning process, we will be better able to provide what is needed to optimize their play.

The toys and props children use in their play are the tools of their trade. In the previous chapter, we discussed the qualities that make do-it-yourself learning toys appealing to providers of early care and education; in this chapter, we will look at their value as learning tools.

As we said before, the children don't plan, organize, or think about their learning; they just do it. Adults, on the other hand, like things broken down into categories. With that end in mind, we have categorized and described some of the major learning that will take place while children explore the activities and materials in this book. There are many things going on during play. Our intention is to give you a broad overview of some of the most important learning that takes place while kids play with these materials. We will look at how the projects in this book will help children develop skills in the following areas:

- Language and literacy
- Math and logical thinking
- Science
- Art, music, and creative expression
- Initiative and social relationships
- Physical skills

There is a lot of overlap between the items on this list. For example, most of the projects in this book help develop visual discrimination, which is basically the ability to notice differences in what is seen. These skills play a predominant role in each of the six areas mentioned above. Children need to be able to discriminate visually to read and write, complete math problems, observe science experiments, mix paint colors, understand the expression on a new friend's face, and catch a ball. Because of this overlap, children who are developing their visual discrimination skills while doing an art project will be able to use those skills in the other areas. Painting a picture helps develop skills needed for writing. Catching a ball helps develop skills needed for reading. Building with blocks prepares a child to learn math skills. This idea of skill overlap and transfer is difficult for many parents, and providers, to understand. The rest of this chapter will help explain what kids are learning while they play and why that learning is important.

Language and Literacy

It is impossible to overvalue a preschooler's acquisition of a rich vocabulary and the ability to use it prior to entering school. Strong language skills are tools children use to acquire more language and information about their worlds. Most children will successfully acquire their primary language by age five, but research seems to indicate that the deeper their understanding of that language, the more successful they will be in school. The most important gift we can give children is the gift of language.

In *At a Loss for Words,* Betty Bardige says, "Humans are social animals, and their children come into the world primed to communicate. Language and symbolic thought, the hallmarks of humanity, develop very early. The first five years of life, and especially the years between one and four, are prime time for language learning" (2005, 21). The projects in this book help adults bathe children in language, preparing them to talk, read, and write.

They will be awash in new vocabulary: *PVC pipe, plywood, sandpaper, duct tape, nylon twine, weaving loom, flagging tape, gravity, motion, spin, moisture, clamp, level, construction, pulley, pendulum, exploration, building, demolition, magnetic field, theory, idea, hypothesis,* and many, many other words will quickly seep into their vocabularies as they play, explore, discover, and ask questions. Playing with projects like the ones in this book offers a chance to enrich and develop the vocabulary of young children in a natural and relaxed way. There is no drilling or worksheets, just conversation and questions. The children will learn language from these activities by talking with you about them, by asking and answering questions.

The conversations that take place in conjunction with the activities are the key; they provide you with a way to share new words and ideas, let children discover meaning through conversational context, and help them develop the following important pre-literacy skills. Meaningful conversation can help children do the following:

- Ask questions
- Listen to and retell stories
- Sequence objects, events in a story, or steps in completing a task
- Be easily understood by others when talking
- Manipulate sounds
- Use inventive spelling
- Follow simple directions
- Identify likenesses and differences
- Identify simple shapes
- Identify basic colors
- Answer simple questions
- Show awareness of environmental print, such as the words they see on fast-food bags and cereal boxes

The best way to learn these important skills is in real-life situations; children learn to talk by talking. As they participate in the activities in this book, they will naturally add to their knowledge of language. Caregivers should make opportunities in their conversations with children to encourage development of the preceding skills. Such intentional conversations can introduce powerful new words that will begin to pepper the children's talk and effortlessly enrich their vocabularies.

In addition to vocabulary, these conversations can build awareness of how the world, and language, works. Caregivers can give language development a huge boost by encouraging children to talk during activities and by asking simple, open-ended questions such as the following:

- How (did you make that, can we fix it, can we make it better, etc.)?
- What (is that, are you doing, happened, happens next, etc.)?
- Can you (do it again, make another one, show me, explain, etc.)?
- Tell me about what you (did, made, saw, think, need, want, etc.)?
- How are they (alike, different, related, used, made, etc.)?

Questions like these will take children to new places, ideas, concepts, and understandings. They will help build language skills and understanding. They will immerse children in new vocabulary.

We also have to make sure we answer the children's questions, and answer them mindfully. Adults all too often tend to brush aside the barrage of questions that flow from young children. It takes time, but answering their questions is a valuable way to expand their knowledge. Remember, "I don't know" is an acceptable answer, but we encourage you to follow it up with the words "but I'll help you find out" whenever possible.

Preverbal children should also be engaged in discussion as much as possible. They cannot talk, but they understand what they hear and they reap huge benefits from being included in conversations. Remember, they learn language by being bathed in language—not just hearing it, but being a part of the give and take of conversation.

Many of these activities also help children develop pre-literacy skills in other ways. Open-ended learning toys allow children to

- improve small-muscle dexterity
- practice visual discrimination
- learn about negative space
- experience rich dramatic play

Small-Muscle Dexterity

The refinement of small-muscle skills is another important component of language and literacy development. Children need to learn to grasp and release objects, manipulate small bits and pieces, and generally master the use of their fingers before they are able to learn to write. Dexterity is a skill that kids must practice. Many of the projects in this book are designed to develop these pre-writing skills. If you cannot manipulate a pencil, you cannot write.

Visual Discrimination

Many projects help promote the development of visual discrimination, a skill needed for reading and writing. *Visual discrimination* is simply a fancy way of saying that you can see differences in similar things. Children need this skill so they can tell a W from an M or a B from an R.

Negative Space

Many of the projects also help children internalize the concept of negative space. This is like learning to see the hole in the donut, the difference between the foreground and background, the difference between the page of a book and the letters on that page. If you cannot visually separate the words from the page, you cannot learn to read.

Dramatic Play

The dramatic play area is usually overflowing with language. Many of the activities that follow can be used in the dramatic play area. In fact, a whole chapter is devoted to items that can enhance your dramatic play area. Children use the dramatic play area as a place to practice language on their own and with peers. You can enhance this learning by stocking your dramatic play area with books, catalogs, paper, pencils, pens, and other items that will help children integrate reading and writing into their play.

In *Play in the Lives of Children,* Cosby S. Rogers and Janet K. Sawyers state, "Although play is not a necessary condition for learning language and literacy skills, play is probably the best environment for these abilities to thrive" (1988, 64). Play and language are inseparably linked. Language skills will grow while children play. As a caregiver, you can use the information above to build a play environment that is richer in language and more conducive to its development in young children as they play.

Math and Logical Thinking

In the preface to *The Block Book,* Elisabeth S. Hirsch says, "The pleasure of blocks stems primarily from the aesthetic experience. It involves the whole person—muscles and senses, intellect and emotion, individual growth and social interaction. Learning results from the imaginative activity, from the need to pose and solve problems" (1996, vii).

Children love to play at solving mysteries and problems; they are fascinated with magic tricks, bringing order to chaos, discovering strange new bugs in the backyard, and trying to unravel all the mysteries of the adult world. Children like challenges. We have designed many of the following projects to take advantage of that desire to rise to challenges. The best part of solving a problem is the inner pride you feel when you have overcome its challenge. Here is an example: We built a small platform and hung it from a hook in the middle of our playroom ceiling. We positioned a baby doll on the platform, placed a tote full of PVC pipes and fittings on the floor, and said to a group of children ranging in age from two and a half to four, "Can you get the doll down?"

A few attempts were made to knock the doll down by tossing pipes. One two-year-old repeatedly tried to jump up and grab the doll. After a while, a bright-eyed four-year-old girl named Libby tried to poke the doll down with a long piece of pipe. She couldn't reach her target.

The younger children saw that she was on to something and took turns poking with their own long pipes. Eventually, Libby added a straight fitting and another length of pipe and took aim again. She was closer but still could not reach. A second fitting and length of pipe did the job. After some poking she managed to knock the doll from its perch. It fell to the cheers of the younger children. Libby smiled with pride. We replaced the doll, and the younger kids took turns using the tool Libby had invented.

Such challenges are valuable on their own, but they are also one way to help children develop their understanding of crucial pre-math concepts like these:

- Spatial relations
- Length, width, height, and weight
- Number and shape recognition
- Sequencing, sorting, and graphing
- Understanding quantitative words
- Sorting by color, shape, size, weight, etc.
- Recognizing and extending patterns
- Understanding directional words (up, down, in, out, etc.)
- Working independently or as part of a group

The chapters that follow, especially Matching, Sorting, and Estimating; Problem Solving; Construction; and Exploring Tools, provide many chances for children to expand their knowledge of the skills and concepts listed above. During the activities, you can use the following tips to enhance their learning experience:

1. Don't give more help than they need.

In *How Children Learn,* John Holt says, "Little children strongly dislike being given more help than they ask for" (1983, 28). In the challenge described above we could have asked, "Can you build a long, straight pipe and push the doll down?" instead of simply placing the pipe tote on the floor. There still would have been a challenge, but we would have robbed them of the lightbulb moment that makes such challenges so rewarding. One of the hardest things for caregivers to do is to step out of the way and let learning happen. Our desire to TEACH gets in the way of the need to let the children learn. Our job is to set the stage and let the kids do the playing, exploring, and discovering.

2. Remember to use your words.

Children need to hear words and ideas many times before they internalize them, making them their own. Make sure you take advantage of the ample opportunities that these activities offer for giving children new words and ideas.

3. Make them feel safe.

Trying new things and testing new ideas is potentially dangerous because these activities involve a step into the unknown, a learning risk. Most adults feel uncomfortable speaking up or sharing a thought in a room full of strangers. They fear that their idea or feeling will be laughed at or discounted. They fear ridicule, rejection, and retribution for speaking their mind.

Kids can feel the same way. That is why it is vital for us to create safe, nurturing, and warm environments where learning risks are encouraged. If children are made to feel comfortable and safe while learning to sort or count blocks at the age of three, they will be better equipped to multiply fractions at the age of thirteen.

4. Give them time.

We will repeat this over and over throughout the book. Kids need big chunks of time that they can use to explore and play as they see fit. You cannot let them spend ten minutes with most of these activities and expect them to be sated. They will long for more time to play and learn; they NEED more time to play and learn. If at all possible let them set the schedule when it comes to how long they spend with an activity.

Science

Math and logical thinking relate closely to our next learning category: Science. Many of the skills listed in the last section also help children prepare to explore the physical world. Children are natural-born scientists; their early years revolve around exploring and making sense of the world around them. They are constantly making new discoveries that help explain how their world works and what their place in it is. You know those scientists who go off and live with apes, gorillas, or lions to learn their ways? Well, newborns are the scientists, and their caregivers are the apes. They come into our world curious to learn how we interact with each other and the environments around us. They observe us, study us, and are eventually accepted into our group.

As good apes, we need to do our best to help these brave young scientists make the discoveries that will help them understand our world. In addition to the concepts and skills we've already talked about, here are some of the things that they need to learn:

- Cause-and-effect thinking
- How the physical world works: the basic ideas of gravity, momentum, energy, mass, and magnetic fields
- How to develop and test a theory or hypothesis
- How to form conclusions based on their observations

The curiosity of these young scientists is relentless and tireless. They are constantly testing and observing and asking "WHY?" It is enough to drive the most patient ape batty. Their quest to discover may nearly push us over the edge sometimes, but we need to do everything we can to promote and nurture this early inquisitiveness. The desire to explore and know new things fades all too quickly from the hearts of too many children.

There are many projects in the following chapters that will help children understand the world better while they play. Here are a couple of things you, as a caregiver, can do to help quench their thirst for knowledge and keep it alive while they play:

1. Remember to breathe.

When a toddler wants to play a sorting game for the two-thousand-six-hundred-and-ninety-third time, when a preschooler lets a block structure crash to the floor again, after you said one more time was enough ten times ago, when you wonder if they will ever stop asking WHY?, take a deep breath (or five or ten of them), be a good ape, and remember that little scientists need to explore. We need to be patient with their need for repetition. It is not easy to do, but it is important to help them through this part of the learning process.

2. Let them make mistakes.

In 1492 Christopher Columbus was looking for India when he found North America. In the late 1950s Wilson Greatbatch grabbed the wrong transistor while working on a device meant to record heart sounds and accidentally invented the implantable cardiac pacemaker. In the 1970s a guy named Spencer Silver was trying to invent a super-strong adhesive when he invented the weak adhesive that makes Post-it notes work. It is rare that mistakes result in great inventions and discoveries, but many, many great lessons have been learned by getting it wrong the first time. Besides, a few early mistakes make later success taste all the better.

3. Observe and respond.

As you observe children at play with these materials, keep an eye out for ways to make the experience more meaningful. It is important to be

responsive to teachable moments when you see them. You may also observe that activities need to be adjusted to meet the individual needs of children. Early learning depends a lot on strong relationships between children and caregivers. These relationships are strengthened when you effectively respond to their learning needs. Don't jump in too quickly to help—just observe and give them what they need.

Art, Music, and Creative Expression

Early learning research indicates that creative activity, such as art, music, and dance, benefits young children by stimulating the brain in a variety of regions. Here are a few of the ways children can benefit from creative activities:

- improved memory
- greater small- and large-muscle control
- creativity that crosses over into other kinds of problem solving
- ability to think about more complex problems and to understand their own thought processes (metacognition)
- increased sense of timing
- development of written and spoken language
- increased spatial reasoning

Art, music, dance, and other creative outlets for young children are about process, not product. Whether they are painting a picture, playing a tune, or performing a play, young artists should be encouraged to fully explore the materials and use them to express themselves as they see fit.

To adults this self-expression may look like colored macaroni glued to a piece of paper. To the child it is a monster, a race car, or daddy coming home from work. It is important to give the children control of their art projects. Encourage them to find their own voice, paint their own picture. Promote unique one-of-a-kind projects, not cookie-cutter replications of adult work.

Too many programs fall into the habit of prefabricating children's creative projects. An adult will cut out the pieces or do the "hard parts" of the project so all the child has to do is color within the lines, glue the pieces together "right," or "play the song like I showed you."

This is not art, it is not creative, and it in no way allows the children to express themselves. Projects should be messy, free, and open ended. Children should color, sing, glue, dance, and paint as they wish within broad parameters. The purpose may be self-expression, exploration of an idea, or understanding how something works, but it is not replication.

Creative activities, done in an open and free way, are more than simply an empowering act of self-expression. Allowing children to express themselves through art and other mediums

- allows children to practice physical and academic skills needed for school

- is often a therapeutic outlet for strong new emotions and a way of reducing stress

- promotes experimentation with, and exposure to, a wide variety of props, materials, and ideas

- gives them another tool for exploring how things work, problem solving, or recording the world around them

Many of the projects in this book use unconventional materials that are usually not associated with preschool art, music, and movement projects. Interactions with these new materials provide sensory experiences that allow children to look at objects and think about them in different ways. These new ways of thinking spur brain activity and development; they have a powerful effect on neural activity, helping wire the brain.

When children use materials in new ways, they tend to use not only their brains but also their entire bodies differently. While they sing, dance, move, and express themselves, they develop small- and large-motor skills that are vital components of their development. Activities like hand clapping, finger snapping, hopping, balancing, and touching the left hand to the right knee actually help build the brain connections needed for more complicated thought and activities. Many of the projects that follow give children chances to create and move— supporting brain building though music, art, and creative expression.

Initiative and Social Relationships

"All intelligent creatures play. The 'higher' the animal, the more prolonged is the play phase of life, the more varied and complex the play. In humans, play is the primary path to learning for the first five years or so."
(Piers and Landau 1980, 19)

This prolonged play phase of life in humans—that first five years or so—is prime time for acquiring new skills, assimilating information, learning how the world works, and testing theories. It is also the time when children start developing their own initiative and the skills needed to manage social relationships throughout their lives.

Whether they are engaged in dramatic play, an art activity, a large group project, or one-on-one time with their child care provider, play is almost always a social activity. While playing, they are busy learning how they fit into and can influence the world. The social side of play helps teach children these abilities:

- Focusing on a task

- Playing and interacting with other children and enjoying being part of a group

- Following simple directions

- Feeling like an able learner

- Sorting and sequencing: being able to engage in play scenarios involves knowing the beginning, middle, and end of the story, "what happens next"

- Asking and responding to questions

- Maintaining voice control

- Taking turns and sharing

- Developing awareness of personal space

- Using words to express needs and feelings

- Showing responsibility

- Showing age-appropriate emotional responses

- Using words to solve problems when angry or frustrated

- Sharing and taking turns

- Learning self-care

- Listening while others talk

- Using strong oral language skills

The social side of play is vital for developing talents and skills that are very valuable to children as they enter school and throughout their lives. The ability to manage their life and their relationships with others is essential.

In *The Youngest Minds,* Ann B. Barnet and Richard J. Barnet say, "Babies have an innate drive to learn and a biological preparedness for emotionally laden social interactions. Anyone who observes normal babies knows that they are often as eager to engage in social play as they are to eat. In a baby, play is learning" (1998, 137). Even with the benefit of this biological preparedness for social interaction, learning to plot a course through the heights and depths of interpersonal relationships is challenging. Adults, with their years of experience and practice, are often uneasy, stressed, fearful, and anxious when it comes to interpersonal relationships. Imagine being a child navigating uncharted social and emotional waters. Imagine the initiative and self-confidence needed to make new friends, take new chances, and walk into new social situations.

The newness of many of the materials used in these projects is a real catalyst for promoting the initiative needed to meet social challenges. Children are born explorers and adventurers; the chance to interact with new things and ideas is very compelling. Most children will take the initiative needed to make play with the new materials happen. These activities will help children develop the confidence they need to take learning risks, to step up and say, "I know," "I want to try," "I have an idea," "Let's try this," or "I don't know." The activities provide safe cover for exploring, testing theories, and building confidence.

We've chatted with many early elementary teachers over the years and found that their biggest struggles in the classroom usually revolve around children with deficient social skills. You have probably met the child: possessive, unwilling to share or take turns, overly aggressive, impatient, and pushy. These are all normal human attributes, and there is nothing wrong with any of them in small doses, but children who are unable to regulate these traits usually spell TROUBLE in the classroom. That is why some of the most important ready-for-school skills young children can develop revolve around playing nicely with others and self-regulating. The best way to develop these skills? Practicing during group play.

Group play, and its attendant social skills, is fostered through adult-led activities and child-directed play. Many of the projects will describe adult-led learning involving taking turns, sharing, group decision making, and other social skills. The social skill development that takes place when caregivers create a play-friendly environment and then step back to the sidelines is profound. Children learn to "use their manners" during play. The micro-society created during group play is very powerful. Most children quickly learn to operate within the social mores established by their peers and the adults in their early learning environment.

The opportunities for dramatic play, problem solving, block play, and other social activities created by these projects are rich occasions for social skill development. This type of play is practice for the adult world. Social play allows children to naturally work on the skills they will need when they one day run that world. Caregivers must nurture this type of play in their programs.

Physical Skills

Picture a two- and three-year-old exploring an inviting environment; they touch, manipulate, and maneuver objects as they flutter around the room. They are tactile, curious, and one part of them or another is always in motion. Their young bodies are designed for motion; telling a two-year-old to sit still is like telling a river to stop flowing. Since movement is such a big part of being a young child, every activity in this book helps develop and fine-tune children's large- or small-muscle skills. Among other things, this movement and muscle development helps children

- develop dexterity
- improve balance
- build coordination
- strengthen muscles and bones
- strengthen the heart and lungs
- improve hand-eye coordination
- teach visual discrimination
- build neural connections
- promote sensory integration
- gather information about their environment

While every activity involves children's physical skills in some way, we have made sure that many of them focus specifically on things like movement, sensory play, and manipulatives. In fact, there is a chapter devoted to each of these topics. Learning how to control their small muscles and integrate sensory input are essential skills.

If you are concerned about possible developmental delays in physical (and other) skills, do not fail to follow up on your concerns. The earlier you deal with such potential problems the better. Some things you should watch for:

- "Good" babies and toddlers who don't move around a lot and who don't get into things

- Older children who lack interest in activities and are unable to concentrate

- Children who will not cross their midline (an imaginary line that runs down the center of the body). For example, you should be concerned about preschoolers who are unable to touch their left ear with their right hand or scratch their elbow

- Delayed smiling, visual alertness, chewing, or babbling

Children should have ample time each day for physical activity so that they can reap the rewards that come from putting their bodies in motion. Too many children are living sedentary lives, which has a negative impact on all aspects of their development. Make time to move.

Conclusion

There is a lot of learning happening when children play, explore, and discover with the materials that follow. To learn more about how this type of child-directed, open-ended play benefits children, we suggest checking out the Web sites of the following organizations:

- The National Association for Family Child Care (www.nafcc.org)

- The National Association for the Education of Young Children (www.naeyc.org)

These organizations work hard to promote quality early care and education, and both offer accreditation programs for interested child care providers.

Each project that follows contains a short paragraph outlining some of the learning that takes place when children engage in that activity. We have done our best to include the primary learning that takes place, but keep in mind that there is usually much more going on under the surface. Children bring their own autobiographies to each interaction; this makes each occasion for play a unique event. Be aware of the children in your care and their own special needs, interests, and ways of learning. Take the time to customize things when needed to help them get the most from the projects.

We started this chapter with the quote "Young children do not differentiate between play, learning, and work" from Rogers and Sawyers. Be mindful of this quote as you proceed through the rest of the book; it could not be truer.

References

Bardige, Betty. 2005. *At a loss for words*. Philadelphia: Temple University Press.

Barnet, Ann, and Richard Barnet. 1998. *The youngest minds*. New York: Simon & Schuster.

Hirsch, Elisabeth, ed. 1996. *The block book*. Washington, DC: National Association for the Education of Young Children.

Holt, John. 1983. *How children learn*. New York: Addison Wesley Publishing Company.

Piers, Maria, and Genevieve Landau. 1980. *The gift of play: And why young children cannot thrive without it*. New York: Walker and Company.

Rogers, Cosby, and Janet Sawyers. 1998. *Play in the lives of children*. Washington, DC: National Association for the Education of Young Children.

3

GETTING STARTED

> Children are naturally flexible in how they grow and learn. So are their brains. They arrive prewired with multiple opportunities for development. They are endowed with the ability to take advantage of many things in many ways. —Craig Ramey and Sharon Ramey, *Right from Birth: Building Your Child's Foundation for Life*

As you can see, the projects in this book have the potential to foster a wide range of learning. The wonderful thing about working with young children is that they will always surprise you. After incorporating these projects into your program, you will find that the children will visualize and build things that are wholly unexpected and exciting. When you delve into the following chapters you will see that each project includes descriptions of the types of learning facilitated, how you can help set the stage for learning, and variations for different ages, settings, or skill levels.

Tools and Materials

One of our goals while writing this book was to make construction of the projects as easy as possible for the average caregiver. With that goal in mind we tried to design as many projects as possible so that they required the same basic tools and materials. The following is a list of items used repeatedly throughout the following chapters:

- Duct tape
- Nylon twine
- Two-sided tape
- Scissors
- Superglue

Cutting

We tried to avoid cutting with anything other than scissors as much as possible. Some projects, however, require the use of bigger tools to cut wood, plastic, and wire. If you are uncomfortable using these tools, or unfamiliar with their use, we strongly recommend that you find someone to help. If you need assistance, ask. We have discussed the use of power tools with many caregivers and found that most providers who are uncomfortable with these tools have spouses, family, friends, clients, or neighbors willing to help with the projects that require them. Table saws and power miter saws are potentially dangerous to inexperienced users, and even those with experience must be very careful. We do not want to scare you away from these projects; we just want to ensure that they are done safely.

Sanding

Sanding is another activity we wanted to avoid. It is easy to do, but it is messy and often time consuming. When you build the projects that do require sanding, make sure you wear a dust mask and proper eye protection to keep your lungs and eyes safe. Do your sanding in a well-ventilated area, outside if possible. None of the projects will require more than some light hand sanding to remove burrs and gently round edges. Power sanders are not needed or recommended. Some projects will require light sanding to help avoid slivers and splinters.

If you choose to allow children to help sand projects, and we recommend that you do, make sure they also have the proper safety equipment. Keep their eyes and lungs safe.

Fastening

Since we strove for project simplicity, most of the fastening in this book is done with different tapes and glues. These are things that most people know how to use and have around the house already.

Finishing

We have avoided any painting, staining, or other finishing. In fact, there is only one project, the light table, that requires any painting at all. We did this for a number of reasons. Finishing projects can be expensive and time consuming. Most caregivers have tight budgets and tight schedules. We don't want you to spend any more time or money than necessary.

Another reason for our no finish policy is that it is not necessarily safe. Finish cans are covered with warning labels. Lingering fumes and potential chipping can be dangerous for young and old alike. If you do not use these products, you do not have to worry about the potential hazards.

The final reason we avoid finishes is that we feel it is aesthetically unnecessary. We want children to interact with the materials as they are; finishes would cover the textures, smells, and other traits of the materials. Bright, shiny, loud finishes would take away from the simple, basic, and calm feeling we want these projects to impart. We are looking for low-key learning, not overstimulated activity.

Keeping Kids Safe While Playing and Exploring

The primary ways to ensure that children are safe while playing and exploring with the materials in this book is to know the children well and keep a close eye on them while they go about their work. Since they are so curious and designed to explore, children will use materials in lots of ways, including potentially unsafe or dangerous ways. Very young children also mouth objects as a means of exploration and this can lead to choking. **Be safe. Keep an alert eye on children at all times.** Curiosity killed the cat and it could possibly do the same to a young child.

That said, we believe that well-supervised children of all ages should be allowed to explore and use small objects, ropes, string, hammers, and hand saws. Children are curious, not suicidal. They want to explore and learn, not do themselves in. Many early childhood environments are too sterile. Many of the items that children need to interact with are banished from the environment in the name of safety. If children are not allowed to learn to safely handle these items in a well-supervised environment, they will miss many wonderful opportunities for sensory and small-motor development.

One of the activities later in the book involves paper clips. While we were shooting pictures for the book in a family-based program a little girl, about age two, fell in love with the brightly colored paper clips we brought. She spent over forty-five minutes picking them up, placing them in containers, sorting them into piles, and generally getting to know them. Not once did a paper clip go near her mouth. Not once did anyone worry about her choking.

The conventional wisdom would advise that the paper clips be kept away from such a young child. The reality is that she had a valuable sensory and small-motor experience. The provider was in tune with the child's abilities, and we were all keeping a close eye on her as she played. We had to pack up our materials and move on before she was done playing. As we walked out the door she was settling down at the kitchen table with a box of shiny new paper clips her provider found in a drawer.

It would have been easy to cheat her of this learning opportunity in the name of safety. Too many children miss out on too many activities because some arbitrary guidelines scare providers and parents away from play deemed too dangerous. Do not give children small objects and lengths of rope and walk away. Know the children, know the materials, and pay close attention at all times. Children can and should safely play with these "dangerous" items in appropriately well-supervised environments. It takes work on the provider's part, but the payoff for the children is huge.

Maintenance

As with all toys and equipment, it is important to perform regular safety checks on your do-it-yourself early learning materials. We have designed durable and long-lasting activities, but they are not impervious to wear and tear. Keep an eye out for potential hazards and correct them before they become problems, rather than waiting for an injury to occur.

Shopping for Materials

The vast majority of the items required to make the projects described in this book are for sale at your favorite local home center. We suggest you bring the book with you to the store if you are unfamiliar with the items required for a project. A store employee should then be able to direct you to exactly the items required.

The price of materials is going to vary in different parts of the country, but we have tried to provide a fairly accurate guess for each project so you will have a general idea of what projects will cost. These estimates are based on what we paid in our community, observed during visits to other communities, and saw while price checking on the Internet. You may be able to find better prices for some items online, but we found that shipping costs ate up any real savings. Our recommendation is to buy locally to support the businesses operating in your community.

Another recommendation is to shop around for deals; many of the materials used in these projects go on sale regularly. We did our best to develop projects that are affordable, but any money you save on materials is money saved. Look for sales, rebates, and other chances to save a few dollars.

There are a few materials that are required for many projects: nylon twine, duct tape, and superglue are the big three. A 200- or 300-foot roll of twine, a roll of duct tape, and a tube of superglue should be at the top of your shopping list.

The most important thing to do when shopping for materials is to bring the children when possible. We understand that transporting children is not always practical or possible, but involving them in the whole process of making new program materials is in itself a great learning experience. It is a wonderful chance for them to go out and visit the adult world, ask questions, and see new things. Helping you purchase materials and then turn those materials into toys is a wonderfully empowering experience for a preschool child. If at all possible make this a part of the project-building process.

Storing Your Creations

We've never worked in, visited, or heard of a child care program that had too much storage space. The fact is most programs have insufficient space to properly store their equipment. With that in mind, we did our best to choose supplies for the activities in this book that were simple to store and did not take up too much space.

The vast majority of these projects can be stored in large resealable freezer bags. We have found that they are the right size, affordable, and durable. If you store the individual projects in a freezer bag, and then store the freezer bags in a large tote, you will be able to keep things organized and out of the way when not in use but still have easy access to them when needed.

Each project includes a suggestion for storage based on how we ended up storing that item in our family child care program.

The Play Environment

For children to benefit as much as possible from these activities, the play needs to take place in a learning-friendly environment. We have to set the scene for children to play, providing the appropriate setting and props for their explorations and discovery. John Holt, in *Learning All the Time,* says, "Real learning is a process of discovery, and if we want it to happen, we must create the kinds of conditions in which discoveries are made. We know what these are. They include time, leisure, freedom, and lack of pressure" (1989, 100). Children need large blocks of time with the freedom and leisure to fully explore materials. Learning for young children is not about pressure, it is about relaxation, comfort, and fun. It is about PLAY. The best way to use most of the materials and activities in this book is to simply put them in front of the children with little or no explanation and stay out of the way. In fact in *The Lifelong Learner,* Ronald Gross says, "Structure the chance to learn, offer feedback and support, provide some tools and ideas, and stay out of the way" (1977, 37).

Staying out of the way is critical. Be there, be attentive, be observant, but stay out of the way. Children need to make discoveries on their own. The experience is not theirs if you take the lightbulb moment away from them. Let them make the discoveries. Let them think, "Aha, that is how it works." Early learning is about children discovering, not adults teaching.

While it is important not to get in the way, it is vital that you stay tuned in to what they are doing. Give children space to explore, but be there for the vital moment-to-moment give-and-take so you can respond to their signals. Know the children well so you can effectively meet needs as they arise.

The most important ingredient to make these activities successful is time. Make sure the children in your care have the ample time they need to freely, and fully, explore the materials. Remember that young children need time to repeat activities. What may look like mindless repetition to adults is learning to young children. Children have to repeat activities until they have integrated them into their thinking and scheme of the world. Give them the time they need to make their own discoveries about how the physical world works.

Aside from the need for pressure-free time to play without too much adult intrusion, children need an environment that is conducive to active, self-directed learning. Learning for young children is usually hands on, often messy, and sometimes noisy.

Creating an environment that encourages free, child-initiated, relaxed, open-ended play is the most important contribution you can make to children's early learning. When they know they have the freedom to explore on their own and that you are there to help when it is needed, they will feel safe taking the risks inherent with new activities and situations.

References

Gross, Ronald. 1977. *The lifelong learner.* New York: Simon and Schuster.

Holt, John. 1989. *Learning All the time.* Reading, Mass.: Addison-Wesley.

ACTIVITIES—EXPLORING GRAVITY AND MOTION

> Children take their first steps toward a lifetime of logical,
> scientific inquiry when they have the freedom to explore as children.
>
> —Cosby S. Rogers and Janet K. Sawyers, *Play in the Lives of Children*

The activities we have put together in this chapter will give children a safe and comfortable opportunity to play with the laws of the physical world as they explore.

These activities usually bring about lots of HOW, WHY, and WHAT IF questions. Make sure you take the time to answer these questions or, better yet, help children discover their own answers when possible. Allow children opportunities to perform experiments and test theories that grow from these activities.

These projects also provide children with great opportunities to add rich new words to their growing vocabularies. Children who integrate words like *pulley, pendulum, gravity, force, energy, projectile,* and *motion* into their personal dictionaries are powerful children. Give the children these words and others related to the activities. They will then be able to use their new vocabularies to ask questions, give answers, and draw more new language into their lives. This is a great opportunity to feed their voracious appetites for new words.

Baby Catapults

Have you ever wanted to help children launch wads of tinfoil across the room but just didn't know how to make it happen? Well, we've got the answer for you right here: Baby Catapults. You'll have all the fun and excitement of a medieval siege without any of the destruction.

Ages
2
and up

Materials

- ☐ Wood, approximately 2 inches wide, 8 to 10 inches long, and ⅛- to ¼-inch thick
- ☐ ½-inch schedule 40 PVC pipe connector
- ☐ Round plastic snap-on milk jug lid
- ☐ Duct tape
- ☐ Superglue
- ☐ Sandpaper, 100 grit
- ☐ Tinfoil

Tools

- ☐ A saw if you need to cut your wood to size

Estimated Build Cost

$5 should purchase a piece of wood big enough to make three or four baby catapults.

Directions

1. If you need to cut a long board into catapult-sized sections, do so now. Then take a few minutes to gently round over all the edges and corners with your sandpaper.

2. The next step is to super-glue a milk jug lid onto one end of your board. This will serve as the payload area, a nice safe place to put your projectile before launch.

3. Now turn the board over and duct tape the pipe fitting someplace between the board's center and the end opposite the payload area. Run thin strips of duct tape through the fitting and around the board's width. This fitting will serve as the unit's pivot point. We tried prettier ways of adhering the fitting, but neither hot glue nor superglue would stand up to the heavy use the prototypes received. Duct tape has worked marvelously.

4. Now that the catapult is built, it is time to make the payload. Simply wad up pieces of tinfoil into little balls. Vary the sizes. You want them between ½ and 1 inch in diameter. You can vary their weight by compressing them more or less. A lightly compressed ball with a 1-inch diameter will weigh less than a ball the same size that is really scrunched together. The variations in size and weight will affect the way the balls fly. Your projectiles are complete!

5. To launch, set your catapult pipe-side-down like a teeter-totter with the payload side on the ground. Place a foil ball in the payload area, press down quickly on the other end of the board, and watch the foil fly. The harder and faster you press the farther and faster the ball will travel.

6. Bring on the children. Demonstrate once or twice and then let them explore the materials. Give them plenty of time and space to experiment and only as much help as they need.

Storage

You can store six or more baby catapults and a bunch of tinfoil balls in a gallon-size freezer bag.

What's Learned

While children are making tinfoil balls fly across the room, they are learning about motion, potential energy, and other physical science laws. They are also learning about cause-and-effect relationships and feeling very powerful and in control.

Variations

- Launch sponges. The sponge blocks from chapter 12 make wonderful projectiles.

- Try to launch items into an ice cream bucket or cardboard box.

- Use a tape measure to see how far objects fly and chart this information.

Radical Ramps

Made for trimming rooms and furniture, cove molding is the perfect shape for this fun and educational activity. Children will love sending cars, balls, and other objects down these versatile and easy-to-build ramps. They will be busy playing, exploring, and experimenting, and at the same time learning about physical science.

Ages
18 mos.
and up

Materials

☐ Cove molding

☐ Small cars

☐ Small balls

Note: Cove molding (and almost all molding) is usually located not in the lumberyard, but in the millwork department because it needs to be maintained at a fairly consistent temperature and humidity to avoid warping. Cove molding can be found in a variety of widths. You may want to consider purchasing a few different widths, if you have adequate storage space.

Tools

☐ Handsaw

☐ Sandpaper, 100–120 grit

Estimated Building Cost

$10 will probably allow you to build all the ramps you could possibly need.

Directions

1. Create a few sections of molding ranging in length from 12 to 48 inches. Most stores sell this molding in lengths 8 feet or longer. You can purchase a big piece and cut it to the desired lengths by yourself with a handsaw; the kids would be happy to help with this job. They could help measure, mark, and cut the longer sections to size. If you're not comfortable doing that, most stores will be happy to cut the lengths you need right there in the millwork department. If you do not have lots of storage space, we recommend a single section, 24 inches long. If you have room for more, offer children a variety of lengths. The more pieces in your collection, the more versatility the children will have in their play and exploration.

2. After cutting to size, gently sand the pieces to remove any sharp or rough edges.

3. To use the ramp, just place the molding, cove-side-up, with one end elevated and the other end on the floor. Let the cars and balls roll. The kids will love to repeat this activity. Give them lots of time to play and explore.

Storage

Store on a shelf or in an out-of-the-way corner.

What's Learned

Children are learning about gravity and the laws of motion while sending objects down the ramps. They are also developing their small-muscle skills and hand-eye coordination while playing. This activity is a great way to learn about cause-and-effect relationships as well.

Variations

- Place the ramp at different angles.
- Stand up blocks at the bottom of the ramp and knock them over.
- Use blocks and other ramps to guide a ball across the floor after it leaves a ramp.
- Try other objects and see how they move, or do not move, down the ramp.
- Can they make a ball travel uphill under its own power?
- Can they make a ball turn corners?
- Challenge the kids to think of new ways to use the ramps in their play.

Weight Lifting

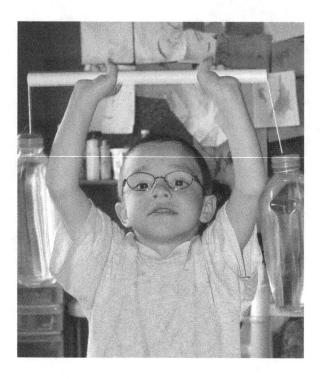

This is a large-muscle activity that the kids will love. We will create a set of kid-sized weights that will encourage youngsters to use the large muscles in their upper bodies.

Ages
2
and up

TIP: You have probably already learned that it is a good idea to build more than one of some projects. This will make sharing easier and help with group dynamics.

Materials

☐ Pipe Construction Set (see p. 184)

☐ Nylon twine

☐ Two half-gallon plastic milk jugs (or similar containers)

☐ Water

Tools

☐ Scissors

☐ Tape

Estimated Build Cost

None

Directions

1. Grab a piece of PVC pipe about 15 inches long from the Pipe Construction Set described on page 184, and thread one end of a 36-inch piece of twine through it.

2. Next add water to the jugs. Fill them about half full, making sure the water level is the same in each jug.

3. After that, all you have to do is securely tie a jug to each end of the twine. Tie the twine through the jug handle, not around the neck of the jug. Also, try to keep the jugs and the pipe as close together as possible; extra twine will allow the jugs to shift.

4. Show children how they can grab the pipe and lift the water-filled containers. Discuss whether it feels heavy or light, whether it is easy or hard to accomplish. Stress taking turns and putting the weights down gently to avoid any big spills. When we built this project, two-and-a-half-year-old Maddie shouted, "It's stronger than me!" as she struggled to lift the weight over her head.

Storage

This project can be dismantled when the children lose interest. It can always be easily rebuilt at a later date.

What's Learned

This is a great way to develop strong arms and backs. Kids love to play at being big, strong, and powerful. This project strengthens their muscles and their sense of self.

Variations

- Vary the amount of water in the jugs.
- Encourage children to count their lifts.
- Graph the number of lifts each child can make.

Fun with Pendulums

A pendulum is simply a mass suspended so it swings freely on an axis. Once you install your pendulum, the kids will have no problem figuring out how to use it in lots of fun ways. The nylon twine we have used for many projects is the star of this one and comes from the hardware department.

Ages
12 mos.
and up

Materials

☐ ¼-inch eyebolt (there are a few types to choose from, depending on your ceiling structure and installation method)

☐ Nylon twine

☐ Duct tape

☐ Plastic bottle (a 16–20-oz. bottle will work great)

☐ Water

Tools

☐ Scissors

☐ Drill

☐ Hammer

☐ Screwdriver

TIP: This activity demands close supervision to make sure the twine doesn't end up around a child's neck and to avoid injuries.

Estimated Build Cost

The eyebolt will cost under $5. Twine will cost a few dollars if you need it, but you should have everything else on hand.

Directions

1. The first thing you need is an attachment point for the pendulum. We recommend installing an eyebolt in your playroom ceiling. It may sound like a big project, but the fact is it should take less than twenty minutes and cost under $5. Besides, you'll need the eyebolt for a few other projects, so you might as well install it now. If you don't know how to do this, ask for help or consult a home-repair book. If you don't want to install an eyebolt, an overhanging tree branch in your yard will also work. Do not tie your pendulum to a ceiling fan or light fixture; this is not safe.

2. After installing the eyebolt, you have to create the mass that will swing at the bottom of your nylon twine. To do this, fill the plastic bottle with water and screw the lid on tight. You can hot glue the lid on if you feel it's necessary.

3. Next, tie the end of your nylon twine securely around the neck of the bottle. After tying, reinforce the connection with duct tape. The last thing we want is for this connection to fail and send the bottle flying across the room.

4. Now secure the other end of the line to your attachment point. You want the pendulum to swing freely. Hang it so that the bottom of the bottle is between 6 and 12 inches from the floor. Make sure the twine is securely knotted at the apex. Give the bottle a gentle swing and see how it reacts.

5. It's fun to just watch the way the bottle moves when swung in different manners. Kids will enjoy experimenting with and observing this motion. The big fun comes, however, when you start knocking things over. Place an empty cereal box on the floor. Swing the pendulum. Crash! Repeat.

Storage

Store your pendulum and twine in a large freezer bag when not in use.

What's Learned

When kids watch the pendulum swing, they will be observing and internalizing the laws of motion. When they swing the pendulum and knock a box across the room, they are exploring physical science and the way objects interact, as well as developing their hand-eye coordination. They are also learning about cause-and-effect relationships.

This is also a very empowering activity for small children. Giving them the opportunity to control the swinging pendulum so it crashes into something is a powerful gift. To learn responsibility, children need to be given power; this is a great way to give them some control over their world.

Variations

- You can build a frame using your Pipe Construction Set and suspend a small pendulum from it for tabletop pendulum play.

- Set up ten boxes like bowling pins and take turns seeing how many tries it takes to knock them down.

- Construct a big building with your blocks and then call in the wrecking ball for demolition.

- Experiment with different amounts of water in the bottle and different twine lengths and see how these variables affect the pendulum's motion.

- Try filling the bottle with fine sand and making a small hole in its bottom. Cover your floor with black paper and watch the pattern that the leaking sand makes while the pendulum swings.

- Another way to make patterns is to cover a cookie sheet with sand and place it under a pendulum made with a weighted stick instead of a bottle. Make sure the stick just touches the cookie sheet's surface so that as the pendulum swings it makes a pattern.

Playing with Pulleys

Here is another reason to have an eyebolt in your playroom ceiling. Children love hoisting and lowering things and will be learning the whole time. This is a great large-muscle and science activity.

Ages
12 mos.
and up

TIP: All kids under the age of 12 love this one!

Materials

☐ Small pulley

☐ ¼-inch rope, 20 to 30 feet long

☐ Ice cream bucket

☐ Hook

☐ Nylon twine

Tools

☐ Scissors

Estimated Build Cost

The pulley, hook, and rope will cost around $10 to purchase. Figure in another $6 or so if you have to eat a gallon of ice cream to get the bucket.

Directions

1. We really hope you have broken down and installed an eyebolt in your ceiling by now. If you have, simply secure your pulley to the eyebolt with a piece of twine. Attach it well.

2. Now string one end of the rope through the pulley. You should have at least enough rope to run from the floor, up to the ceiling, and back to the floor; 5 to 10 feet more is even better.

3. Leave one end of the rope alone. Securely fasten your hook to the other end and then attach the bucket to the hook.

4. With the bucket sitting on the floor, pull the rope so that the bucket makes its way to the ceiling. This is a lot of fun if you're between the ages of two and ten. To make this even more fun you have to put something into the bucket, of course. At our house, baby dolls and blocks are the cargo of choice, although lots of other things have made the trip to the ceiling. Let the kids experiment with different items; just make sure they don't overload the bucket.

5. The first thing most kids do when they get the bucket up to the ceiling is let go of the rope and watch it crash to the ground. Let them do this a few times with an empty bucket; they need to experiment with the materials, and this is a great way to explore gravity. It is part of the learning process. After a few times, ask if they can stop the bucket before it crashes. Children will be delighted (and empowered) when they learn to let the rope slide through their fingers while the bucket plummets only to clamp down and stop it right before it hits the floor. Younger children usually start out holding the end of the rope and walking backward while the bucket rises from the floor. It takes them a while before they realize they can stand in one place and pull the rope hand over hand to raise the bucket.

6. Again, kids and rope can mean danger. Supervise them well at all times when involved with this activity.

Storage

Store the pulley and rope in the bucket when not in use.

What's Learned

Children are learning the scientific concepts of gravity, motion, kinetic energy, potential energy, and mass while lifting and lowering stuffed bunnies. They are also developing their large- and small-motor skills, hand-eye coordination, knowledge about cause-and-effect relationships, vocabularies, and a sense of themselves as powerful individuals. There is a lot going on in this activity!

Variations

- Like the pendulum, you can build a tabletop version. Use a PVC pipe frame, smaller pulley, yogurt container, and twine.

- Tie a 6- to 10-foot section of twine to the handle of the ice cream bucket so that one child can guide the bucket to a new location while another lowers it. This adds a whole new cooperative learning facet to the activity.

- Remove the bucket and attach other items to the hook.

- The kids in our program discovered this variation; we call it "keep away from the toddler." All you do is attach an interesting item to the hook and let any child over three use the pulley to keep the item just out of reach of a toddler. We have seen nothing but joyous laughter every time the kids have done this at our house.

Things Are Spinning Out of Control

Behold the lowly 5-gallon bucket lid. Nothing fancy; it is round, plastic, and not much more . . . until you start playing with one and take the time to realize all the possibilities.

Ages **12** mos. and up

Materials

A 5-gallon bucket lid, but it has to be the right kind. What kind is the right kind? Well, what you are looking for is a lid with a small dimple (about 1½ inches in diameter) in its center. The right bucket lid will have a dimple that sits below the outside rim so that it revolves on the dimple-point if you spin the lid. The spinning is the key. Make sure any potential lid is a good spinner. Get down on the floor and try it out in the store if you have to, because no spin means no fun.

Tools

None

Estimated Build Cost

Many home centers sell 5-gallon utility buckets with their store name and logo printed on the side for a few dollars, and you can purchase the matching lid for around $1. You may also be able to recycle a lid from a 5-gallon bucket of paint or plaster; just make sure you clean it well. Again, it has to be the right kind of 5-gallon bucket lid to work.

Directions

1. The fun comes when you give the lid a spin and then drop something—like a wad of tinfoil, a block, a plastic cow, or a crayon—onto it. If the lid is spinning fast enough, the object will fly off; if it is spinning more slowly, the object will settle onto the lid for a ride. If you try it once, you will not be able to help trying it a few more times, and you are an adult. Imagine how much the kids will enjoy experimenting with different items. Demonstrate with a few objects and then encourage them to try bits and pieces of different size and shape. Younger children will not have the dexterity to spin the lid well, so you may need to spin while they drop items. Help out only as much as is needed.

Storage

Bucket lids will store easily on a shelf or in a tote when not in use.

What's Learned

They don't know it, but children are working as physicists when they repeatedly spin the lid and drop items. They are discovering the laws of physics for themselves, learning how objects in motion interact. They are also developing their motor skills and learning about cause-and-effect relationships. All this learning takes place while simply playing with a bucket lid.

Variations

- Use the lid as a lazy Susan for markers and other items during arts and crafts time. Kids can easily rotate the lid to reach the items they need.

- Add a lid or two to your dramatic play area. They will become serving trays and other play props.

- Spin a lid on its edge for a whole new physics lesson.

Watch Out for Flying Marshmallows!

We don't generally encourage children to play with food, but when we discovered that miniature marshmallows fit perfectly into the end of a piece of PVC pipe, we had to make an exception. There are few things more fulfilling than projecting a miniature marshmallow across a room with a quick puff of breath. Okay, for grown-ups there are too many things more fulfilling than air-powered marshmallow projection to name, but it is at the top of the heap if you're a kid and you get to eat a few marshmallows now and then during the activity.

Ages
18 mos.
and up

Materials

☐ Pipe Construction Set (see p. 184)

☐ Miniature marshmallows

Tools

None

Estimated Build Cost

You will spend around $2 for the marshmallows, depending on how many you go through.

Directions

1. Grab a 10- or 12-inch piece of pipe per child from the Pipe Construction Set described in chapter 15.

2. Demonstrate how to place a marshmallow into the end of the pipe and then blow through that same end. The marshmallow will fly based on how hard and quick you blow. Kids love this activity.

3. Make sure you stress that they should not inhale, only exhale. Sucking in a marshmallow probably wouldn't do them any harm, but it is better to be safe than sorry.

4. There are probably people reading this who are thinking that there is no way they are going to allow the humid breath of children to propel wads of sugar across their playroom; you adults may want to restrict the fun to the outside play area.

Storage

The pipes all come from one tote. Just put the pipes back in their storage tote.

What's Learned

While projecting marshmallows across the room kids experience the properties of objects in motion and pneumatic power. This activity also improves hand-eye coordination and is a great workout for growing lungs.

Variations

■ Set up targets to aim for; ice cream buckets work well. See who can get the most marshmallows in the bucket from five, ten, and fifteen paces. You can then graph the results.

■ Discuss how our lungs work.

■ Discuss other ways we use air pressure to complete tasks.

■ Challenge kids to use the pipe set to build a tube that will project a marshmallow around a corner.

Let the Good Times Roll

Young children will enjoy repeatedly sending marbles racing down these flexible tubes. This activity is easy to prepare and will engage children for quite a while. It is good, clean, repetitive fun.

Ages
2
and up

Materials

☐ Flexible electrical conduit, 10-foot section

☐ Tape measure

☐ Marker

☐ Duct tape

☐ Marbles

Flexible electrical conduit—the words just roll off your tongue. This stuff is great. It has a nice blue color (we've seen other colors on the Internet, but never in person), will stay in almost any shape you can bend it into, and it is ribbed, so it has a neat

> **TIP:** Younger children will need close supervision because the marbles are choking hazards.

> **TIP:** Count your marbles before and after the activity to make sure they all make it home safe and sound. If not, you can send out search parties for any missing pieces that could become choking hazards. Remember, there is always a chance of choking when you mix small children and small manipulatives.

texture. It usually is sold in 10-foot sections, but you could probably get a 200-foot roll if you really like the stuff. We use this stuff in a few projects throughout the book.

Tools

None

Estimated Build Cost

The section of flexible electrical conduit should cost less than $2.

Directions

1. This activity does not take much more than one cut, a few bends, and a little duct tape. Measure and mark the center of the conduit and then cut the long section in half.

2. Now bend and twist each half a little bit. You are trying to make some curves and turns for the marble to follow as it descends through the tube.

3. The last step in preparation is to tape one end of each conduit to a table or chair leg and let the other end descend to the floor. The chutes are now ready for marbles. This project works best with wood, linoleum, or tile floors because they allow the marbles to keep moving when they leave the tube. It is also a good idea to aim the bottom of the tube so the marbles do not head under a chair or buffet when they exit the tube; we learned this from experience.

4. The only thing to do now is give children some marbles and let them experience and explore the activity. You may need to adjust the bends in your pipe, or its starting height, to get the marbles to fly down the tube. The kids will love the activity and soon think of many ways to personalize it.

Storage

These items are a bit tough to store. Keep them flat on a shelf if you have room. They can be looped and taped together if that makes them easier to store.

What's Learned

This activity and its variations teach about cause-and-effect relationships, physics, and problem solving, and develop motor skills and hand-eye coordination. It will also help younger children grasp the concept of object permanence as they see the marble enter the tube and reappear at the bottom.

Variations

- Rest the bottom of the tube on a chair seat so the marbles fly off into space after exiting the tube. Can the children determine where to place a bowl or box to catch the flying marbles?

- Mark an X on the floor with tape and challenge older children to use blocks to guide the marble to this point after it exits the tube.

- Let the children put the bends and twists into the tubes.

- Tape the tubes together side-by-side to create a double-barreled marble raceway.

- Put the marbles away and then try some water (you might want to do this outside).

Spiderweb Tape

It's amazing what you'll discover if you goof around with masking tape long enough. This project will allow kids to make objects almost defy gravity while they play and explore.

Ages
2
and up

Materials

☐ Roll of 1-inch masking tape

☐ A variety of small toys, manipulatives, and scrap paper

☐ An open doorway

Tools

None

> **TIP:** One of the best items to use with this project is construction-paper scraps.

Estimated Build Cost

$1 will buy you a roll of tape that will allow you to repeat this project a number of times.

Directions

1. Collect your manipulatives and grab your roll of tape. The doorway you select needs to be accessible to the kids and in a safe location. The doorway at the top of a flight of stairs is a bad idea; the doorway to your play area would be great.

2. Now simply run strips of tape across the doorway at a variety of angles so the sticky side faces the side where you want the children working. When you get done it should look like a giant spiderweb made of tape. Make sure you put the tape up while the children are watching.

3. The questions will start flowing. What are you doing? (I'm putting tape across the doorway.) Why are you putting tape there? (It's for a project.) Can I touch it? (Yes, please do.)

4. You will have their undivided attention. All you have to do now is ask them what they think will happen if you stick something to the tape, a Hot Wheels car for example. Let them toss out a few hypotheses and then do the experiment; stick the car to the tape. What happens?

5. Now ask if they want to take turns trying other items. They will. Have them start out with the items you selected, but encourage them to think of other items to try. This activity is all about exploration, observation, and experimentation. Let them try items you know are too heavy or too large to hang from the tape; children learn as much from things that don't "work" as they do from their successes.

6. Once the children are done sticking the paper to the tape, you can clean up by simply crumpling everything up and tossing it in the trash.

Storage

Store your tape collection in a gallon-size freezer bag.

What's Learned

Children will learn about scientific inquiry, about asking "what if . . ." questions. They will learn to develop and test a hypothesis. Every time they pick up an item to stick to that spiderweb of tape, they will be testing and discovering science.

Variations

- This project can also be done by stretching the tape between two tables with the sticky side down. This will give kids a completely new experience and another situation to explore.

- Use tape of different widths and types; duct tape, electrical tape, and blue painter's tape.

- Chart which items stick or do not stick.

- Time how long heavier items will stick before they fall.

5

ACTIVITIES—MATCHING, SORTING, AND ESTIMATING

Learning to discriminate visually is an important part of learning to decode written language. Young children need to practice telling different shapes, colors, sizes, and textures apart. This practice will not only help them notice and appreciate the subtle differences in the world around them, it will help them learn to recognize the differences in letters on a written page. This is a skill that takes time to develop, and a great way to get that practice is through matching, sorting, and estimating activities. Children should have many opportunities to practice and hone these skills in a variety of ways.

Another benefit children will garner from these activities is the ability to make educated guesses. They get a chance to practice analyzing available information and making informed guesses based on that information. These guessing, estimating, and remembering activities are a great way to develop and practice skills that they will use their whole lives. These games help develop the skills needed to do everyday adult tasks like estimating when it will be time to buy milk, organizing a kitchen cabinet, or sorting laundry. They also lay the groundwork for complex thinking skills, mathematics, and decision making.

These children's games are really powerful tools that teach valuable skills they will be able to use throughout their lives.

Keep Them Guessing

Have you ever tried to guess what was in a wrapped package by shaking it as you carefully listened? This is a fun and easy way to re-create that activity and encourage children to make predictions based on their observations. A sealed paint can could contain almost anything! What does it sound like when you shake it? Is the can heavy or light? Does it make noise when you don't move the can?

Children will love to guess the can's contents almost as much as they will love the suspense of opening the can for the big reveal.

Ages
2
and up

Materials

☐ Paint can and lid, quart or gallon size

☐ Found items to put in the can

Tools

☐ Paint can opener

TIP: This activity is appropriate for any child with enough language to make a guess.

Estimated Build Cost

You can purchase a new empty paint can and lid for $2 to $4, depending on the size.

Directions

1. This is almost too simple. Place an object the children know in the can when they are not looking and firmly press on the lid.

2. Now have them take turns manipulating the can and guessing what it might contain.

3. After everyone has made a guess, open the lid and let them see what was inside. We have seen three-year-olds actually shake with anticipation and excitement as the lid is removed.

4. With younger children, you may want to give them choices before they guess. Ask something like "Is there a block or a ball in the can?" Then have them shake and turn the can before making their guess. Limiting choices will make it much easier for children to succeed at guessing. Ask younger children things like "Does it sound like a rock or a feather?" This will help them focus on a few possibilities and increase their chance for success.

Storage

Store your can in a closet or tote. You can even use it to store other equipment when not in use.

What's Learned

This is a great activity for helping children learn to make predictions based on limited information and past experience. Children will also work their small-muscle skills as they manipulate the can and use their senses of hearing and touch to collect information to make their guesses.

Variations

- Remember that these cans were made to hold liquid. Try using warm or cold water or even ice in the can.

- Let the children hide an object in the can so you can guess.

- Teach older children how to use the can opener so they can play on their own. It will give them ownership of the activity and control over the game.

- Introduce written language into the game by writing down the guesses that are made. It is important for children to see the writing process as an important part of the adult world.

A Simple Matching Game

The little cardboard paint samples you find displayed in any paint department are great for creating custom matching games for the children in your care. Paint sample cards offer endless variety, and best of all they are usually free for the taking.

Ages
2
and up

TIP: If you feel guilty taking paint samples when you have no intention of buying any paint, do one of the following: Let the person working in the paint department know you work with young children and need the samples for a project; they are usually very eager and willing to help. Or pick up paint samples for a project you have been putting off, and use these samples with the kids after your painting is done.

Materials

☐ A variety of paint samples, two of each color you select

Tools

None

Estimated Build Cost

None

Directions

1. The most important part of this project is selecting the right sample cards. The long rectangular ones with five or six colors will work okay, but they are not ideal. The cards you want are the ones with one color that usually measure around 2½ inches square. These are perfect for our activity. These cards will have a solid color or will maybe demonstrate a painting technique or application process. Select two each of six to twelve different cards.

2. There are two basic ways to use these cards. You can play Memory with a small group of children by placing the cards color-side-down on a table and then taking turns looking for matches. The person with the most matches wins.

3. The other way is to divide the cards into two piles so that both piles have one of each card. Then one person puts down a card and the other person puts down his or her match. This is a great one-on-one activity for children who need some help with their matching skills.

Storage

Store these items in a gallon-size freezer bag.

What's Learned

The meat of this activity is visual discrimination, learning to compare and contrast visual images. This activity will help children develop the visual dexterity needed for reading and other visual activities.

Variations

- For more advanced children you can create card sets using shades of one color. This will challenge their ability to differentiate between subtle color differences.

- Use laminate, tile, or carpet samples instead of paint samples. This will also introduce the kids to some different textures.

A Superdurable Matching Game

Children love matching and memory games, but the cardboard versions don't usually stand up to heavy wear and tear. Taking a moment to transform a few of the blocks you'll build in the Domino Block Set (see p. 194) will give you a long-lasting matching game. The best part about it is its versatility; you can customize the game to the interests of the children with which you work.

Ages
18 mos.
and up

Materials

☐ 24 domino blocks

☐ Stickers

Tools

None

Estimated Build Cost

If you already have the blocks, this project will cost you only a few dollars for the stickers.

Directions

1. First you need the blocks. Check out page 194 for instructions.

2. The construction of this project revolves around putting pairs of matching images onto the blocks. We tried a variety of methods and found that the easiest is to use a set of cute stickers. Make sure they will fit onto the blocks and that they come with multiples of each image. Another thing to check is their stickability; you want them to stay stuck when you stick them. Some manufacturers make their stickers easy to remove so parents can peel them off the floor, refrigerator, or cat. We want stickers that stick. Make sure you choose stickers with images that the kids will enjoy.

3. Here's the sticky part. Once you have your twenty-four blocks and twelve pairs of matching stickers, all you need to do is put the stickers on the blocks. You've done it. You've created your own superdurable personalized matching game.

4. You can use them in a variety of ways. You can line them up sticker-side-down and play Memory. You can also arrange them sticker-side-up for another game. Select a block and ask a child to find its match. Repeat until all the blocks are paired. You can also just leave the set on a table. The children will build with them, invent their own games, and discuss the images.

Storage

Store your game pieces in a large freezer bag.

What's Learned

This is a great activity for teaching visual discrimination. For younger children, choose stickers that are very different. This will make differentiation easier. Older children will want more of a challenge because they are able to identify differences in images that are similar. For them, choose stickers with subtle variations.

Variations

■ Make sets of three matching blocks instead of two.

- Use photos from your program. With a digital camera and computer you can use images of things the kids see every day. Adhere the pictures to the blocks with spray adhesive. Photos of the kids themselves are a big hit.

- Put two smaller images on each block to make a domino set.

- Use alphabet or number stickers to promote language development. You can also use the kids' names.

Matching Nuts, Washers, and Bolts

Matching bolts, washers, and nuts is a fun, hands-on way to learn about similarities and differences. Manipulating the pieces is a good small-muscle activity for little fingers. Kids will also enjoy working with these materials because of their novelty.

Ages
2
and up

Materials

☐ Assorted nuts, bolts, and washers

Tools

None

Estimated Build Cost

Purchasing the materials for this project should cost you under $10.

Directions

1. When purchasing materials for this project, make sure you are shopping somewhere that sells nuts, washers, and bolts by the pound or by the piece. You do not want to shop somewhere that only sells them by the package; you don't need that many of any one size. What you should concentrate on is variety. Look for bolts that range in diameter from ¼ inch to 1 inch and range in length from 1 inch to 6 inches. Make sure you are purchasing carriage bolts, not lag bolts; the shaft of a carriage bolt stays the same diameter from head to tip; lag bolts come to a point so they can be anchored into wood. To spice things up a bit you can toss in some machine screws of different sizes too. Once you have your bolts and screws selected, purchase matching washers and nuts.

2. Introduce a small group of children to the materials. Let them feel and manipulate the pieces. Share the names of the different pieces and discuss their size, shape, and texture. You can also discuss how adults use these items to build things and hold things together.

3. After they have become familiar with the items, demonstrate how to thread a nut onto a bolt. Show them how to use their fingers to twist a nut up the bolt's shaft. Now ask them if they can match the bolts to the appropriate nuts and washers. Give them time. Provide just the right amount of help; encourage them to figure things out for themselves.

This project is about children making their own discoveries.

Storage

We found that an ice cream bucket makes a wonderful storage container for this play set.

What's Learned

This activity provides an opportunity to explore hand-eye coordination, develop small-muscle control, discriminate visually based on size and shape, and have a tactile experience with the materials.

Variations

- Purchase multiples of some nuts and bolts and then use them for sorting.
- Dig out your measuring tools and measure your collection of bolts.
- Drill some holes in a piece of wood and let the kids thread bolts into the holes and then attach them with washers and nuts.
- Have children sort the nuts and bolts into categories such as long or short, thin or wide.

Sorting Seeds

Sorting seeds is a great way to promote visual discrimination, hand-eye coordination, and small-muscle skills in young children all at the same time. This is important because those skills are all vital components of emergent literacy.

Ages
3
and up

Materials

☐ Seeds, five or six different kinds. We recommend large seeds such as squash, peas, beans, or sunflowers.

☐ Small containers. We used plastic baby food containers.

☐ Large container and lid. We used a cottage cheese container.

Tools

None

Estimated Build Cost

Seeds are usually $1–2 a pack, but at the end of the growing season you can get them at a huge discount.

Directions

1. Not much preparation needed here; just dump all your seeds into the large container. The children can then sort the seeds into the smaller containers.

2. You might want to help out less-experienced sorters by placing a seed or two in each container so they know what goes where. It is also a good idea to discuss the textures and other properties of the seeds as you sort. Start a discussion about which seeds have stripes, which ones are bumpy, which ones are smooth, color differences, etc.

3. Beginning sorters will also be more successful if you start them off with only two types of seeds. They can work up to more varieties as they gain expertise.

Storage

We made sure our seeds and small containers all fit into the large container for easy storage. Just stick it on a shelf or in a tote until you need it.

What's Learned

This sorting activity will teach children to discriminate visually, to tell the difference between items based on their appearance. This is a skill that they will call upon as they learn to read and write. Visual discrimination is how we tell the difference between an A and an R. This activity also develops small-muscle skill, building fingers strong and nimble enough to master the use of pencils, scissors, and other tools.

Variations

■ Sort seeds by color or texture instead of type.

■ Blindfold children so they can try to sort seeds by touch alone.

■ Challenge older children to think of other ways to classify the seeds.

■ See if children can create letters and numbers from the seeds.

Learning to Estimate

This activity will help children develop their ability to make estimates based on observation. It is a simple activity for small groups or individual children.

Ages
3
and up

Materials

☐ Nuts, ¼-inch diameter

☐ Bolts, ¾ inch long, ¼-inch diameter

☐ Two glass baby food jars

Tools

None

Estimated Build Cost

Try to purchase your materials by the pound—it will be cheaper. Expect to pay around $10 for the needed items.

Directions

1. Here is another easy one. Just put some nuts in one jar and some bolts in another, and screw on the lids. It is best to start with fewer items in the jar. Give the children chances for success and increase the challenge as you play.

2. Next, let a few children turn, twist, and manipulate the jars. Ask them to guess how many pieces are in each jar and record their guesses.

3. Open one of the jars and start to count the pieces. After counting a few items, ask them if they would like to revise their estimates. Write down any adjustments they make before you finish counting. Compare their estimates to the actual number. Repeat for the other jar.

Storage

These items will store nicely in a large freezer bag.

What's Learned

During this activity, children will be learning about estimating and making educated guesses. This is the basis for the scientific practice of making, revising, and testing a hypothesis. They will also gain some very basic understanding of the concepts of volume, mass, and weight as they interact with the materials. They are setting the groundwork for scientific understanding.

Variations

■ Make sure you vary the number of items in the jar each time. Use different-sized containers each time you play.

■ Put nuts and bolts in the same jar.

■ Combine different sizes of nuts or bolts.

■ Allow the children to fill the jars and do the counting while you guess.

6

ACTIVITIES—PROBLEM SOLVING

The activities in this chapter build on the skills children developed in the last chapter on matching, sorting, and estimating. These projects encourage children to think and act in more complex ways as they practice following directions, solving problems, copying patterns, and completing tasks. The following projects are open-ended opportunities to help children expand their thinking skills, acquire new language, practice working as part of a group, use their prior knowledge, make predictions, and gain more knowledge about the physical world.

When you use these activities, think of the children as young scientists and engineers hard at work solving problems. Give them the time, space, and freedom needed to build their own solutions to the problem at hand. Give them autonomy; let them make their own mistakes, reach their own conclusions, and be successful in their own ways. These projects are not about you being the smart adult showing them how to do something. These projects are about the children discovering their own solutions to problems. The best thing you can do to promote this process is to set the stage and then step out of the way, involving yourself only when truly needed.

Sink the Cork

What could be more fun than water, corks, and kids? In this activity, kids will experiment to determine how much weight it takes to sink corks of different sizes. The activity can be adjusted to fit the needs of children of different developmental levels.

Ages
2
and up

Materials

☐ Corks, assorted sizes

☐ Small screw-in hooks

☐ Clear container 6 to 12 inches deep

☐ Water

☐ Washers, assorted small sizes

Tools

None

Estimated Build Cost

You should be able to purchase the corks, washers, and hooks for under $10.

Directions

1. The only preparation needed for this activity is to screw some hooks into some corks. The corks are very easy to screw the hooks into because they are so soft. It does not matter where you install the hooks on the corks; try to use some variety. There is no need to make them all the same.

2. Now fill your clear container about three-quarters full of water.

3. The activity is simple. Drop the corks into the water and see them float. Now add a washer to the hook and try the cork again. See how many washers it takes to make the cork sink. If possible, purchase a variety of very small washers. If you get washers that are too large, the cork will sink quickly—smaller washers are better. Demonstrate this for the kids.

4. Let the kids play and get to know the materials.

5. After they have acquired some knowledge of the materials, have children guess how many washers or paper clips it will take to make their cork sink. Give them a chance to revise their estimates after each attempt.

6. Now have them try a different-sized cork and make a new estimate.

7. This activity works best if the kids are given plenty of time to get their hands wet and explore and discover on their own.

Storage

You guessed it: store these items in a large freezer bag.

What's Learned

With this activity, children will learn about fluid dynamics and buoyancy. They will also learn about making predications and adjusting those predictions based on their observations. Kids will need lots of time to play and experiment with the materials; they are scientists working in their laboratory.

Variations

- Use paper clips instead of washers.
- Have older children chart their predictions.

- For younger children, just playing with the corks in the water may be enough.
- Use warm or cold water or add some food coloring.
- Try to suspend other items from the hooks.
- Attach two corks together with a paper clip and see how much weight you need to add to make them both sink.
- Try to make the cork "hover" between the top of the water and the bottom.

Building People Sculptures

This project is a great outlet for pent-up artistic energy. It will dramatize how the human skeletal system holds our bodies up, as well as the importance of good balance and posture.

Ages
3
and up

Materials

☐ Pipe Construction Set (see p. 184)

☐ Old newspapers

☐ Clothing

☐ Medium-sized paper bag

☐ Markers

☐ Tape

Tools

None

Estimated Build Cost

None

Directions

1. You may want to build an example for younger children; older kids should be fine with some basic instructions. Our daughter, Zoë, pulled this project out of her well-fertilized imagination when she

> **TIP:** This activity is appropriate for children 5 years and up, if doing the activity independently; 3- and 4-year-olds will enjoy it with help.

was about nine years old. What we are trying to build is a stylized but life-size person. Your Pipe Construction Set (page 184) will serve as the skeleton. The old newspaper will flesh things out; use it to stuff the clothing and give your dummy some dimension. The newspaper-filled paper bag will make the head. Then just add a face with the markers and tape it to the PVC neck bone.

2. Start at the ground and work your way up. Build your person to fit the clothing your mannequin will model.

3. Good posture and balance are important if you want your creation to stand on its own. This will take time, effort, and possibly a big pair of shoes stuffed with newspaper. Have fun and experiment with different poses. You will not be able to build too many people with one Pipe Construction Set unless you add more pipes and fittings.

Storage

No need for storage; just put the pipes back in their totes.

What's Learned

This project is great for self-expression and experiencing the joy of creating. Children will also experience and internalize lots of information about gravity and other physical science principles.

Variations

- How about adding hair? Or background scenery? Or writing a story or song involving the pipe people you have created?

- Instead of people, build animals, maybe a horse or T. rex.

- Another possibility is to forget the clothes altogether and build the most detailed skeleton possible. PVC ribs, anyone?

Copying Patterns

This activity is very similar to the previous one in that it encourages children to follow directions, but it takes things a bit further by challenging them to identify and replicate patterns. Pattern recognition is essential in learning to read and write. This activity will help them develop the skills needed to read a blueprint or schematic and put together a home entertainment center when they are adults.

Ages
3
and up

Materials

☐ Pipe Construction Set (see p. 184)

☐ Note cards

☐ Pen

Tools

None

Estimated Build Cost

None

Directions

1. Before presenting the activity to the children, you will need to develop a set of construction diagrams. You do not have to be an artist; just draw some simple shapes that children can construct using the pieces in your Pipe Construction Set.

2. For children new to this activity, you may want to use a different color of ink for each type of fitting (black for straight pipe, red for a 90-degree elbow, etc). This will help them understand the diagram better.

3. When you have a few diagrams ready, ask the children to select one and challenge them to make a duplicate. You may need to walk them through the first few cards, but children who are ready for this activity will catch on quickly.

Storage

Secure your pattern cards with a rubber band or clip and keep them in a gallon-size freezer bag.

What's Learned

The major learning focus of this project is the children's ability to recognize and replicate patterns. They will also improve their ability to visualize an object in three dimensions. This ability is a huge part of reading and writing, an indispensable literacy skill. Children will also develop their skills in following directions and their small-muscle skills.

Variations

■ Vary the intricacy of your diagrams.

■ Make it a group activity to promote cooperative learning.

■ Encourage children to create their own diagram cards to challenge each other.

■ You may also want to photograph things the children build and make the prints available as "blueprints" for duplicating the originals.

Making Tools to Complete Tasks

This project will challenge children to use their creativity and logical thinking skills to solve a problem or complete a task. It is a great way to get them to flex their minds and expand their thinking.

Ages
3
and up

Materials

☐ Pipe Construction Set (see p. 184)

☐ Stuffed animal or doll

Tools

None

Estimated Build Cost

None

Directions

1. When you prepare for outside playtime on a warm spring morning, take a moment to place a stuffed animal or doll on a tree branch 2 or 3 feet over the heads of the children.

2. Place the Pipe Construction Set on the ground nearby.

3. When the children enter the play area, explain that the stuffed animal is stuck in the tree and ask them if they can help think of a way to get it down. The first suggestion will probably be to throw

things at it until it falls. Praise the idea, but try to direct them toward the pipes. Someone will come up with the idea to make a long pipe and "poke" the animal down; see if it works.

4. Soon there will be a line of children with their own animal pokers waiting their turn to rescue that poor stuffed animal.

Storage

No need for storage; just put the pipes back in their totes.

What's Learned

Logical thinking, cooperation, physics, spatial relations, and problem solving are all a part of this activity. The challenge of this activity requires many children to think in new ways and use different strategies for problem solving. This activity can be very empowering and builds self-esteem and confidence.

Variations

- Have them create a tool that will retrieve a ball from under the couch or a pillow from a high shelf.

- Discuss other tools that people use to solve problems.

- Ask the local fire department to stop by and demonstrate how they would save someone stuck way up high.

- Introduce new materials and new problem-solving challenges.

- Ask children to draw a picture of a tool or machine they would like to invent.

Building from Directions

This activity utilizes the Pipe Construction Set from Chapter 15 to develop listening and language skills as well as help children learn to follow directions. This is a fun way for preschoolers to develop these important skills.

Materials

☐ Pipe Construction Set (see p. 184)

☐ Note cards

☐ Pen

Tools

None

Estimated Build Cost

None

Directions

1. First, consider the age of the children you are working with. Use simple verbal instructions with younger children and use added complexity and written instructions with older children.

2. During your preparation time, think of a bunch of tasks the children could do using the pipe set.

3. Now list the tasks on individual note cards. Here are some examples:

- Build a straight pipe as tall as you are.

- Build a letter "E."

- Build a letter "H."

- Build something using three elbows and four straight pipes.

- Build a dog.

- Build an airplane.

4. Have younger children pick a card from your deck, follow along as you read what it says, and see if they can follow the directions. Older children can read the cards themselves and follow the directions. With younger children, it's best to use this activity with individuals or very small groups. With older children, you might want to consider some of the variations listed below.

Storage

Secure your direction cards with a rubber band or clip and keep them in a gallon-size freezer bag.

What's Learned

This project gives kids a chance to hone their small-muscle skills while building their listening, language, and cognitive skills.

Variations

- Divide them into teams and hold a Building from Directions relay race.

- Have them work cooperatively.

- Introduce a stopwatch and see how fast they can complete their tasks.

- Develop multistep directions.

- Have the kids write the directions for you to follow.

- Add other materials and consider increasing the level of complexity for the tasks.

Terrible Twine Tangle

At its heart, this is a great problem-solving activity with lots of variations that will allow many repetitions. What could not be fun about challenging kids to figure out how to untangle yards and yards of twine wrapped around your play area?

Ages
2
and up

Materials

☐ Nylon twine

Tools

☐ Scissors

Estimated Build Cost

This project will cost only a few dollars and you should be able to use it over and over again.

Directions

1. What you want to create is a huge tangle of twine weaving in, out, around, over, under, through, and by everything in your play area. Make sure you choose a play area that is safe for this activity; you wouldn't want to wrap around grandma's antique oil lamp or your new flat-screen TV.

2. To start, just tie the end of the twine spool to a table leg or something similar and start making a mess. Weave it in, out, and around the room's furnishings.

3. When you are done, it should look like a huge spider web engulfing the entire room. Keep the ages and developmental level of the children in mind. The mess you make for three-year-olds will not be the same as the mess you make for schoolagers. Leave the other end of the twine free. Do all of this without any children present.

4. The best part is seeing their eyes bug out when they see the mess. Tell them that an elf, a baby dragon, or your dog made the mess. Explain that you started untangling things but were getting pretty discouraged. Ask for help. Having an adult ask for help is profoundly empowering for a young child. They will be eager to help clean up this mess. This is best done with a very small group; too many kids increases the chance of conflicts.

5. Ask your eager helpers to take the free end of the twine line and start rolling it up. They will have to follow the twine's path and maneuver the spool as they go. Make sure you are nearby to help them if needed, but encourage them to do it themselves. Avoid stepping in and taking over. This is a challenge and should be demanding and feel like hard work. You want them to feel like they have really accomplished something when they finish.

6. Praise them extravagantly when they complete the task. Thank them for their hard work and put the twine away so that elf, dragon, or troublesome dog won't make another mess (until you want them to).

Storage

Keep your collection of twine in a large freezer bag.

What's Learned

This activity promotes cooperative social skills, hand-eye coordination, small-muscle dexterity, and advanced thinking skills. The power the children feel while helping solve a problem for an adult is a huge part of this activity. Children need opportunities to be confident, thinking, self-assured problem solvers. Make sure you provide these opportunities. The children will also have their imaginations engaged by the story you spin to explain the mess.

Variations

- Use two or three twine lines of different colors to increase the challenge.

- For a huge challenge, use multiple lines that are the same color.

- Have one group of kids make the twine tangle, and challenge another to do the untangling.

- Do the activity outside.

- Use two different colors of twine and challenge teams of older children to race to untangle their lines.

7

ACTIVITIES—MANIPULATIVES

The human hand is amazing. Among other things, it bends, twists, lifts, pushes, pulls, pinches, grasps, holds, pats, claps, snaps, rubs, points, motions, and tickles. It is one of the things that make humans so unique. The hands of young children are always in motion, and for good reason. The hand is an important tool that children must master and learn to control. The hand is a very elegant and complex tool that takes much practice to develop and master.

The manipulatives in this chapter are meant to help children develop their hand's skills. They will get a chance to practice movements, learn to grasp fine items, develop a sense of how much grasping pressure is needed to hold different items, strengthen muscles and tendons, and feel confident with this important tool.

One of the goals of all this work is communication. Each time a child plays with one of the manipulatives in this chapter he is developing abilities that are related directly to communicating in print, whether they are writing or typing on a keyboard. Children do not start to learn to write when they enter kindergarten or preschool; they start to learn to write the first time they grasp something in their hand as an infant.

Make sure the children in your care have plenty of time to use these items. It takes time and practice to master these manipulatives and their little hands.

Stitching Their Way into Literacy

Lacing is a great pre-reading and pre-writing activity. It helps prepare the hands and eyes for the tasks of reading and writing. This project is a simple, and inexpensive, way to bring lacing activities into your early care and education program.

Ages
2
and up

TIP: You may want to consider splitting the cost of this project with other providers. It doesn't cost much for the materials or take much time to cut the pieces, but who needs 72 lacing boards?

Materials

☐ Peg board, ¼-inch

☐ Duct tape

☐ ⅛-inch diameter nylon rope

Tools

☐ Table saw (and someone experienced in its use)

☐ Scissors

Estimated Build Cost

A whole 4-by-8-foot sheet of peg board will cost around $12 and make 72 lacing boards. Most home centers also carry it in quarter or half sheets, which will make 18 or 36 lacing boards, respectively. The ⅛-inch diameter rope can be purchased for a few cents a foot.

Directions

1. Unless you are comfortable using a table saw, find someone willing to do the cutting for you. It should not take more than thirty minutes to cut a whole sheet of pegboard into lacing boards. What you want to create is boards that are about 8 inches square. You will need to compensate for the width of the saw blade. That will mean the pieces will actually be around 7⅞ inches square. The big thing to keep in mind when cutting is to keep all cuts centered between the peg board holes. Peg board will differ slightly from manufacturer to manufacturer and from sheet to sheet, so whoever does the cutting will have to make adjustments as needed.

2. To prepare the laces, cut your rope into two 3-foot sections and use duct tape on the ends to create aglets to make the laces easier to hold, manipulate, and negotiate through the peg board holes.

3. There should not be much need for instruction. Just place the materials in front of the children and demonstrate how to lace the rope though the holes. Younger children may need some help manipulating the lace. Let them explore and work with the materials; give them plenty of time for this activity. Some children may prefer to unlace boards that you have laced up before they take on the challenge of lacing.

Storage

You can easily store up to eight boards and a bunch of laces in a one-gallon-size freezer bag.

What's Learned

This project is all about hand-eye coordination and small-muscle skills. This is a great pre-writing activity. It really prepares the hands for holding a pencil and the eyes for recognizing patterns and shapes.

Variations

- Use different media for lacing—ribbon, wire, nylon twine, pipe cleaners, etc.

- Challenge the children to lace letters or numbers.

- Let the children sew boards together. Can they stitch six boards into a cube?

- A family provider using these lacing boards in her program informed us that the children started using the board and laces to practice shoe tying.

Flexible Fun Rings

The biggest charm of these fun rings is their flexibility. You can customize them for different activities and ages. Among other things, children will love to shake them, toss them, rattle them, roll them, and sort them.

Ages
12 mos.
and under

TIP: Make sure the beads or other items you string onto your rings will stand up to the wear and tear young children will give them. Do not use beads that could easily be broken by strong teeth or a fall to the floor. Some of the items we have used are small pieces of PVC pipe, flexible electrical conduit, nuts and washers, and milk jug lids. The kids will know how to use them and will probably think of all kinds of new ways to play with them.

Materials

☐ 12-gauge solid insulated copper wire

☐ Beads or other found items for stringing

☐ Duct tape or electrical tape

Tools

☐ Wire cutters

☐ Pliers

Estimated Build Cost

You can purchase enough wire to make dozens of these rings for around $5. Spend as much or as little as you like on beads or other items to string on the rings.

Directions

1. Cut a section of wire around 12 inches long.

2. Now use your wire cutters to strip around 1 ½ inches of sheathing from each end. String any beads or other items onto the ring at this time.

3. Close the ring by using your pliers to bend a hook on each end of the exposed copper wire and then link the hooks together. Use your pliers to crimp each hook closed, securely coupling them together.

4. If you choose, wrap this connection in duct tape or electrical tape. The wire is flexible so the children can bend them but they are easy to return to their original "ring" shape.

Storage

Your fun rings will store nicely in a gallon-size freezer bag.

What's Learned

The learning that takes place with these items depends on how they are used, but the variations listed below will help children develop their small- and large-muscle skills, hand-eye coordination, cause-and-effect thinking, logical thinking, language skills, creative thinking, and many other abilities.

Variations

- Make a set of eleven rings with zero through ten beads. You can use these for a variety of counting and sorting activities.

- Make a ring with some old keys. In fact, you might want to make a couple of these rings; kids love keys.

- Make four or five rings of different sizes so children can roll them across the floor or spin them on their fingers.

- These rings are great props to add to your dramatic play area.

- Use them for ring toss or try to toss them into an empty ice cream bucket from a few feet away.

- Cut a bunch of 16-inch pieces of fluorescent marking tape. Tie these strips to a ring to make some fun pompom-like shakers. These are great for dancing.

- Make a set of rings, each with beads of different sizes, colors, and/or materials for sorting.

Sticky Manipulatives

When we found Velcro plant ties at the home center, we knew we had to discover some way to use them with the children in our family child care program. We have seen this ½-inch wide green material in rolls 30 or 75 feet long. Made to train vines and other plants, it has microscopic hooks on one side and loops on the other. We use it as a fun and engaging manipulative.

Ages
12 mos.
and up

Materials

☐ Velcro plant ties

Tools

☐ Scissors

Estimated Build Cost

A 75-foot roll of this material costs around $6, and a 30-foot roll goes for under $4.

Directions

1. It could not get much simpler. Just cut the roll into sections ranging in length from 4 to 12 inches. Pieces shorter than 4 inches are easy to lose and are a greater choking risk. We found that children would start using sections longer than 12 inches as whips, and there is also a greater risk of strangulation with longer lengths.

2. To begin play, just show the children how the pieces will stick together in different ways; they'll take it from there.

Storage

Like so many other items, we store these manipulatives in gallon-size freezer bags.

What's Learned

This is another great sensory activity that allows children to explore new textures and materials. The flexibility of the pieces encourages different uses and creativity. Like many other projects, this one works the children's so-very-important small-muscle skills.

Variations

- Play with these manipulatives in the water.
- Stick them to clothing or other fabric.
- Use the pieces to create letters and numbers.
- Sort them by size.
- The pieces stick great to felt boards.

Wire Sculptures

We found that sections of wire make a fun and versatile manipulative that will help train the small-muscle skills of young children. Kids will love to bend, twist, and intertwine this malleable material to form sculptures.

Ages
12 mos.
and up

Materials

☐ 12- or 14-gauge solid insulated copper wire, 10 to 20 feet

Tools

☐ Wire cutters

Estimated Build Cost

$5 should buy all the wire you need.

Directions

1. Just cut a variety of wire lengths; it could not be simpler. We don't recommend making pieces less than 4 inches long or more than 12 inches long. Shorter pieces are easy to lose and are a choking risk. Children are more apt to find creatively inappropriate ways to use very long pieces. No need to measure precisely; just cut twenty to thirty pieces in a variety of lengths. Since these wire sections are so flexible, there is a risk of strangulation; supervise children well.

> **TIP:** This activity is appropriate for children 12 months and up; well-supervised if under the age of 3.

2. To use, just put the wires in front of the kids and demonstrate how to bend and twist them. Children will find all kinds of things to do with these simple manipulatives. Give them time to explore and play with the materials.

Storage

Store your wires in a gallon-size freezer bag.

What's Learned

These manipulatives are great for promoting large-muscle skills and hand-eye coordination. Children who are more experienced players will think of ways the wires can be integrated into their dramatic play. The flexibility of the material will also bring out the creative side of children; this is a great way to promote artistic self-expression.

Variations

- Very small children can explore the materials while sitting in a high chair. Give them a few sections of wire and supervise them well.

- Challenge older children to write their names using the wire.

- Use the wires for sorting.

- Show the children how to construct different geometric shapes using the wire.

- Make and display wire sculptures.

Flexible Manipulatives

Here we are going use flexible electrical conduit (see note on this material under the activity Let the Good Times Roll in chapter 4) to make some manipulatives that are great by themselves or when added to your block or dramatic play areas.

Ages
2
and up

Materials

☐ Flexible electrical conduit, 10-foot section

Tools

☐ PVC pipe cutter or hacksaw
☐ Tape measure
☐ Marker

Estimated Build Cost

One 10-foot section of flexible conduit should cost you under $2.

Directions

1. All you need to do is cut the long piece of pipe into smaller sections. If at all possible, use a PVC pipe cutter for this job. You will be making lots of cuts, and the cutter will make them faster and cleaner than a saw.

2. We made a bunch of 1½-inch, 3-inch, and 4-inch pieces and then a few longer sections. All you have to do is measure, mark, and cut. If you do not have a tape measure handy, just count the ribs on the conduit. Same number of ribs means same-sized pieces.

3. To play, mix the pieces with children and stay out of the way. The kids will quickly find that the blue conduit sections make outstanding pillars when building with the blocks and are great props for use as food or money in the dramatic play area. They will also start slipping them on as "finger extenders." They will also find the longer sections are great for whispering or shouting through. In the beginning, the kids will like these items because they are novel, but as time goes by, they will continue to play with them because they are so versatile.

Storage

Store the pieces in a large freezer bag.

What's Learned

These little tubes have many uses, and that means lots of learning. The children work their small-muscle skills all the time they are using these props and may develop their listening skills, logical thinking skills, language skills, and a host of others while incorporating these objects into their play.

Variations

- Cut very short sections and use them as stringing beads.

- Combine the conduit sections with the sponge blocks (see page 148). The different colors and textures are lots of fun.

- Make them available in your dramatic play area. Children will find all kinds of uses for them.

Fun Manipulatives for Busy Fingers

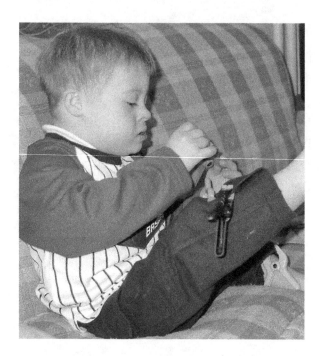

These small plastic clamps are a magnificent manipulative for busy little fingers. They are sortable, sculptable, countable, and even clampable. Make them available and give the kids a chance to explore. The first day the clamps were out at our house, one three-year-old spent over forty-five minutes getting to know them.

Ages
18 mos.
and up

Materials

☐ Small plastic clamps

Tools

None

Estimated Build Cost

We found containers of twenty-two clamps for under $4 and we purchased two. Expect to find similar pricing in your area.

Directions

1. The only preparation for this project is to purchase the clamps. We have seen them in bright fluorescent colors and in basic black. Buy the colored ones if you have a choice. They are more versatile and fun. These small clamps usually are available in affordable bulk sets.

2. Children will begin exploring as soon as you put the colorful clamps in front of them. All you really have to do is make something available to which they can attach the clamps. We've had great luck using cardboard boxes and plastic containers as clamping surfaces. They won't have to squeeze the clamp jaws open too far and will have better success than they would clamping to a thicker surface. The children we have shared these manipulatives with are very eager to explore the items. After getting to know the materials, the children quickly find ways to integrate the clamps into their play.

Storage

We found that a coffee can or ice cream bucket makes ideal storage for these clamps because the children can also use the container's rim as a place to attach clamps.

What's Learned

These handy, dandy little clamps are great manipulatives because they not only help children learn differentiation and discrimination but also they are a great tool for working the fine-muscle control of the hands and wrists that are so vital in mastering the skill of writing. The strength children develop while squeezing clamps open and closed and the agility that grows from precisely placing the clamps prepares them for controlling crayons, pencils, and markers. Many kids will want lots of time to explore these manipulatives until they feel some sense of mastery. Make sure you give them the time they need for this process.

Variations

- Sort the clamps by size and color.

- Use them with your blocks or other manipulatives. The children in our program had a lot of fun with the clamps and the sponge blocks described later in the book.

- While visiting a child care center, we noticed a pair of children using the clamps like forceps to pick up paper clips. The children in our program soon discovered this activity too.

- Show the children how to use the clamps as clothespins in their dramatic play.

- Young toddlers don't have the finger strength to open and close the clamps, but they can enjoy them anyway—just attach a couple clamps to their clothing. They will soon be hard at work trying to remove the clamps.

Tied Up in Knots

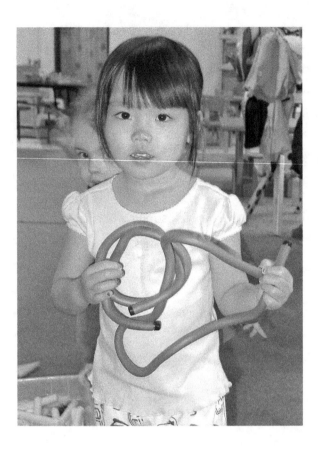

Kwicktwists are 32-inch long wires covered in foam rubber. They are made as tie-downs, an alternative to ropes, straps, and bungee cords. What makes them useful as a manipulative is the fact that they are bendable, twistable, and shapeable. Children will love to manipulate these items and will think of all kinds of ways to integrate them into their play.

Ages
12 mos.
and up

Materials

☐ Kwicktwists

☐ Superglue

Tools

None

Estimated Build Cost

Generally, a pair of these tie-downs will cost you around $6. We suggest you buy a pair, and if you like them you can add to your collection over time. The more you have, the more you can do.

Directions

1. The Kwicktwists' end caps are removable so that they can be connected together to form longer tie-downs. If you plan to let children under age four use these items, we strongly suggest that you super-glue the end caps in place before introducing them to the children. That is the only prep work this project requires.

2. To begin use, just show the children how they can bend and twist the tie downs. Better yet, let them discover these attributes on their own. They will think of all kinds of innovative ways to use these items in their play.

Storage

A set of six or eight will fit nicely into a large freezer bag.

What's Learned

Children will use their fine- and large-motor skills while manipulating the pieces, and they will use all kinds of imagination while bending and twisting. We have seen children turn them into snakes, fire hoses, necklaces, and many other items.

Variations

- Play with the Kwicktwists in the water.

- Use them with the Pipe Construction Set or the flexible conduit manipulatives. The tie-downs fit nicely inside both types of pipe.

- Shape letters and numbers with the Kwicktwists.

Manipulatives That Are a Zip to Use

With a simple modification, cable ties, also known as zip ties, make a great manipulative for encouraging the development of small-muscle skills and hand-eye coordination. Children will enjoy threading the ties together to form all sorts of interesting doodads.

Ages
2
and up

Materials

☐ Cable ties

Tools

☐ Toothpick

Estimated Build Cost

You should be able to purchase a variety pack of cable ties for under $10.

Directions

1. Cable ties are meant to close and stay closed; once you zip them together, they are not supposed to come apart. We have to modify that feature before we can put them in the hands of the children as manipulatives. Luckily, this is simple to do. There is a small tab in the opening of each tie's head that catches on the striations on the tie's tail to lock it in place. To disable this locking mechanism, simply use a toothpick to push the tab out of place. This will create a wider opening, allowing the tie's tail

to move freely in both directions. It will take only a few minutes to do this to all the ties you intend to make available to the children.

2. Once the tabs are disabled, just show the children how the cable ties can be connected together, fastened around objects, and hooked together to make chains. They will soon be experimenting with the ties and finding innovative ways to make use of them.

Storage

Store your assortment of cable ties in a large freezer bag when not in use.

What's Learned

These manipulatives promote the use of small-muscle skills and hand-eye coordination and help to refine those skills. Children will also do a lot of thinking and experimentation while they explore these unique objects. The newness of these playthings will encourage new thinking and creativity.

Variations

- Allow children to use the cable ties with the lacing boards described in the Stitching Their Way into Literacy section earlier in this chapter. Threading the ties through the holes in the peg board is a great way to challenge their small-muscle skills.

- Use ties of different sizes and colors so they can be used in sorting activities.

- Add cable ties to your next water play session. The water will not hurt them, and the children will enjoy the freshness of this activity.

8

ACTIVITIES—KIDS IN MOTION

The activities in this chapter are meant to get children moving. A 1997 article in the journal *Pediatrics* reported that a growing percentage of four- and five-year-olds are overweight. The article recommends that children eat right and get "adequate amounts of physical activity" in their preschool years since lifelong behavior patterns may begin to form at this time (Ogden 1997).

Sadly, too many children are leading sedentary lives, never getting adequate amounts of exercise. Today's preschoolers spend unprecedented amounts of time sitting motionless in front of computers, video games, and television sets. The activities in this chapter are a great way to encourage active play that will help promote a healthy lifestyle.

When using these activities, you can promote healthy living by discussing how our bodies need exercise to stay fit and work properly. Discuss how physical exercise makes our muscles, hearts, lungs, and minds stronger. Use these activities as starting points to promote ongoing health and wellness in your program.

References

Ogden, Cynthia L., et al. 1997. "Prevalence of overweight among preschool children in the United States, 1971 through 1994." *Pediatrics* 99:e1.

Balance Beam

What could be more fun than being three years old and walking across a balance beam with your friends? This is a very simple-to-construct, very durable, and very easy-to-use piece of equipment that the kids will love. It's a great way to challenge their developing muscles and balance.

Ages
12 mos.
and up

Materials

☐ 5-foot section of 4-inch Schedule 40 PVC pipe

☐ Two 4-inch Schedule 40 PVC wye-fittings (this fitting looks like a huge version of the tee-fitting in the Pipe Construction Set described in chapter 15)

Tools

None

Estimated Build Cost

It will cost around $20 to build this project and it will last forever.

Directions

1. It can't get a whole lot easier than this. Just push a wye-fitting (use the perpendicular hole) onto each end of the pipe. What you end up with should be a long and skinny capital letter "I" lying on your

> **TIP:** Any child brave enough to attempt a walk across can enjoy the balance beam, regardless of age.

floor. The wye-fittings stabilize the pipe and keep it from rolling. Project built.

2. Put the balance beam on the floor in your play area, and use will be almost instant. To avoid problems, let the kids know that the balance beam stays on the floor and that they must take turns crossing.

Storage

This is a tough one. We keep our balance beam in a corner by the treadmill where it is out of the way until needed. It would also store easily under a bed or couch. If you plan to keep yours outside, it will stand up to all kinds of weather, so just set it out of the way when not in use.

What's Learned

Learning balance and coordination is the primary focus of this activity. Children also acquire social skills, learn how to follow directions, practice taking turns, and have a chance to encourage their friends as well as be praised by their peers.

Variations

- Add appropriate background music.

- Consider adding some grip tape (the kind that you see on stairs and skateboards) to the beam's surface. It will help make balancing easier.

- Discuss gymnastic events and gymnasts and then create your own Olympic competition.

- Take the balance beam to the outside play area. In fact, this might be a great home for your beam since it will be perfectly fine exposed to the weather.

- For a more challenging activity, construct this piece of equipment from 3-inch pipe and fittings.

- Make noises, the funnier the better, into one of the pipe openings.

- Suspend the balance beam between two chairs and cover it with a blanket or tarp to create a fun and cozy kid-sized tent.

Flexible Conduit Rhythm Sticks

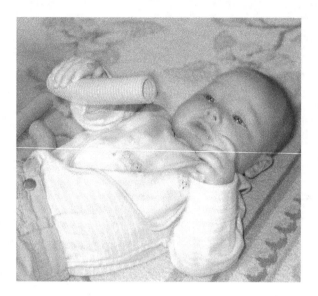

Here is another great way to use affordable and durable flexible electrical conduit. Kids will love exploring the variety of sounds they can make with these instruments.

Ages
12 **mos.**
and up

Materials

☐ Flexible conduit, 10-foot section

Tools

☐ PVC cutter or hacksaw

☐ Tape measure

☐ Marker

TIP: If they can hold them, they can play them.

Estimated Build Cost

You'll spend around $2 on the flexible conduit.

Directions

1. One 10-foot section of conduit is enough material for five sets of rhythm sticks. Construction is simple. Use your PVC cutter or hacksaw to cut two pieces of each of the following lengths: 10, 11, 12, 13, and 14 inches. Get ready to make some music because construction is complete.

2. Let the children choose two pipes each. They do not have to be the same length. Encourage them to bend and twist the conduit into a shape they like, and demonstrate the sound made when striking the two pipes together. There should be some variety because the different length combinations will produce different sounds. The bends in the conduit, as well as where the strike makes contact, will also cause sound variations. Encourage them to explore different ways to make conduit music. This project can be done with a large group, but to really hear the nuance in the sounds a small group is better.

Storage

Store these rhythm sticks in a freezer bag or tote.

What's Learned

While exploring these materials children will be learning about how sound is made as well as working their listening and small-muscle skills. This activity also provides an avenue for artistic expression. This takes time. Make sure they have ample free time to explore and use the materials.

Variations

- Rub two conduit sections together to produce a different sound.

- Try rubbing a rhythm stick's ribs with a pencil to make a new sound. Now try it with a toothpick and any other objects lying around.

- Look for new ways to make sound—try placing a marble, or a few grains of rice, in a tube and shaking it back and forth with your hands covering the ends.

Moving to the Music

Plastic shower-curtain rings are the key to these great props that are wonderful for self-expression as children listen to their favorite CD or audiotape. You can make the rings up ahead of time yourself or construct them with the children's help. Kids will love them, and the best part is that they are affordable and easy to store.

Ages
12 mos.
and up

Materials

☐ Shower curtain rings
☐ Colored ribbons, ¼ to ¾ inch wide

Tools

☐ Scissors

Estimated Build Cost

Materials to make these props should cost around $5.

Directions

1. There are two steps in making this play prop. The first is to cut the ribbon to length. Cut a bunch of pieces 18 to 36 inches long.

2. The second step is to securely tie four or five ribbons to each ring. Just center the ribbons on the ring and knot them a few times. You're done with construction.

3. Use is even easier. Let the children choose a ring or two and then turn on some music. They will almost instinctively start shaking the ribbons as they dance to the music, but you can show them how if they need the help. They probably will not. Let them dance.

Storage

For easy storage, slip the rings onto an empty paper towel tube and keep them near your other musical props.

What's Learned

Dancing and shaking these ribbons is a great way for children to exercise their cardiovascular systems and large muscles. These are things most children do not do nearly enough. It is great for them to get up and make their little hearts pound. The physical and psychological benefit of exercise is as important for children as it is for adults.

Dancing and moving with these ribbon rings is a great opportunity to encourage children to cross their midline (an imaginary line dividing their body in half). Picture a line running from their belly button to the tip of their nose. Ask if they can touch the ribbon ring to their opposite shoulder, elbow, etc. Research shows that this type of activity promotes brain development and that the inability to cross this imaginary line is an indicator of possible developmental problems.

This activity is about creative self-expression as much as it is about exercise. We should encourage children to articulate their feelings, ideas, and thoughts in a variety of ways. This activity is a great way to encourage this expression.

Variations

■ Add bells to the ribbons to make them even more expressive.

■ Discuss the various colors and textures of the ribbons.

- Place a couple of the ribbon rings in the dramatic play area for use as props. The children will find a creative way to integrate them into their play.

- Let some children shake the rings while others make the music.

Ring Around the Child

These easy-to-make activity hoops are a great way to get kids moving. They will enjoy spinning, rolling, and shaking the hoops and will think of all kinds of ways to integrate them into their play.

Ages
12 mos.
and up

Materials

☐ ½-inch plastic drip irrigation hose

☐ ½-inch wooden dowel

☐ Electrical tape

☐ Duct tape

Tools

☐ PVC pipe cutter

Estimated Build Cost

A 3-foot dowel will cost less than $1, and you can get 50 feet of irrigation hose for around $6. This is enough material to make over a dozen hoops.

Directions

1. Cut a section of hose between 30 and 50 inches long with your PVC pipe cutter.

2. Use the same cutter to snip off a section of dowel about 2 inches long.

3. Wrap a 3-inch piece of duct tape around your 2-inch dowel.

4. Inset the tape-covered dowel halfway into one end of the hose section. It should fit snugly.

5. Attach the other end of the hose to the dowel.

6. Cover the connection site with a piece of duct tape.

7. Wrap a layer of electrical tape over the duct tape.

8. Make as many as you want. We suggest you make a few different sizes so the children have some variety when playing.

9. These hoops can be rolled across the floor, spun in place like tops, tossed like a Frisbee, twirled on wrists and ankles, and used in a number of other ways. Show children how to do some of the things mentioned above and let them explore the materials. They will discover many ways to make these hoops part of their play.

Storage

You can store many hoops on a hook in your garage or storage area.

What's Learned

The activity hoops are wonderful props for engaging children in active play. Depending on how they are used, they promote fine- and large-motor development, hand-eye coordination, and balance. Children will also learn about cause-and-effect relationships as they spin, twirl, and toss the hoops.

Variations

- Make a large hoop to be used as a Hula Hoop.

- Place a few grains of rice, or other small objects, in the hose before closing the circle to create a musical hoop.

- Place a hoop on the ground and have children attempt to toss beanbags into it from a distance.

- Lay out a series of hoops and challenge children to hop from one to the next.

- Use the hoops with other materials to create obstacle courses.

- Use hoops as bases when playing kickball.

- Attach shower curtain rings, flagging tape, or other items to the hoops to spice them up a bit.

Rattling and Rolling Toddler Toy

It will only take a few minutes to make this durable and entertaining toy that infants and toddlers will love to shake, rattle, and roll.

Ages
12 mos.
and under

TIP: Some older children find this interesting as well.

Materials

☐ Quart-size metal paint can, empty and clean

☐ 1- by 2-inch magnet

☐ Found items to put in can

Tools

☐ Paint can opener

Estimated Build Cost

A quart-size paint can will cost under $1 if you need to purchase one, and you can get a pack of two magnets for $2 to $3.

Directions

1. If you are employing a used paint can for this project, make sure the label is completely removed and that the can is completely cleaned of all paint residue. Most home centers sell new cans and lids for a few dollars if you don't have an empty one lying around.

2. Once you have a clean, empty can in hand, place your magnet on the inside of the can's side, not on the bottom. This will cause the can to move eccentrically when rolled across the floor.

3. The next step is to put something into the can to make some noise. You want the children to hear something when they roll and shake the can. As an adult, you probably don't want too much noise, so we recommend items like toothpicks, tinfoil balls, rice, wadded paper, or cereal. On the other hand, the children would enjoy items like stones, screws, marbles, and pennies. You make the choice that works for you.

4. Now securely attach the lid and get ready to play.

5. Infants and toddlers are drawn to the can's bright metallic surface and will be eager to explore the new item. Show them how it rolls across the floor and makes noise when shaken. They will enjoy the coolness of the can, the strange sounds they can make, and the amusing way the can rolls across the room.

Storage

Just stick the can with your other infant/toddler toys when not in use; it does not take up too much space.

What's Learned

This is a great toy for promoting small- and large-muscle skills, hand-eye coordination, environmental exploration, and cause-and-effect relationships in infants and toddlers. They will also benefit from the audio, visual, and tactile sensory experiences that are key components of this activity.

Variations

- Change the items in the can every month or so to keep the toy exciting.

- Take the magnet out (or add more) for a different sensory experience.

- Try sealing 4 to 8 ounces of water in the can before play. This will make the can move and sound completely different. Use either cold or warm water for other sensory experiences.

Making Music to March By

If you build the Pipe Construction Set described in chapter 15, this activity will happen on its own, so we might as well prepare you. Soon after introducing your Pipe Construction Set to the children, someone (you probably have the name of the child on the tip of your tongue) is going to blow, sputter, or yell into a pipe. The marching band is born! They will play on and on and on and . . .

Ages
12 mos.
and up

Materials

☐ Pipe Construction Set (see page 184)

Tools

None

Estimated Build Cost

None

Directions

1. There is a good chance you will not have to do anything to prepare for this activity. The children will most likely invent it on their own. When they do, just join the fun. Go with the flow for as long as your ears and nerves will allow. Challenge them to play loud or soft. Encourage them to build the best instruments they can imagine. Experiment with them to see how many different sounds they can create.

2. The other thing the kids will discover on their own is that the pipes make great rhythm instruments too. They can be whacked against each other, empty ice cream buckets, sidewalks, and almost everything else.

3. If you feel like you have to do something, grab your own instrument and teach your band how to march and play at the same time. When the children grasp the marching band concept, step out of the way and let them play. Encourage crossing the midline while marching; show them how to twist their bodies when they march so their instruments move from side to side.

4. To keep your pipes clean, periodically pour a weak water-and-bleach solution (1/4 cup of bleach to a gallon of cool water) over your pipe set while in its plastic tote. Let it soak a while and then drain and allow the pieces to air dry.

Storage

No need for storage; just put the pipes back in their tote.

What's Learned

Among other things, children learn about sound, harmony, air movement, vibrations, rhythm, how much noise their caregiver can tolerate, and having fun. They will also develop large- and small-muscle groups, learn to work with their peers, and develop the self-confidence to perform in front of others.

Variations

- Instead of making noise into the pipes, encourage children to listen to what things sound like when holding a pipe to their ear. You want to avoid any loud noises directly into the pipe, but the sounds of whispers or ambient noises are fine.

- Can they build one "horn" that two or more children can play at once?

- What happens if they blow into a pipe while the other end is in a bucket of water?

Hopping Hurdles

Inside or out, this very physical activity is a great way for young children to get their hearts pumping and test their agility. It doesn't require much preparation or setup and is great for a group or with an individual child.

Ages **18** mos. and up

Materials

☐ Pipe Construction Set (see page 184)

Tools

None

Estimated Build Cost

None

Directions

1. Select the needed materials from the Pipe Construction Set described in chapter 15.

2. Select two T-fittings and insert a 4-inch pipe into each of the three holes; these are the hurdle feet and risers.

3. Now, grab a 15-inch piece of pipe and attach a 90-degree elbow to each end so the open holes face in the same direction; this is the hurdle cross section.

4. Next attach a riser to each open elbow hole to complete a basic hurdle. You can change the length of the riser pipes to alter the height of the hurdle.

5. Build two or three more.

6. The best way we have found to introduce this activity is to set up a series of hurdles (leave about 2 feet between them) and start stepping over them ourselves. A line of interested children will quickly form and you can take turns going over the hurdles. Just stepping over them will be a challenge for many young children; some will be able to hop or jump over. Let the children direct the course of the play from this point.

Storage

No need for storage; just put the pipes back in their totes.

What's Learned

Large-muscle skill development is the primary focus of this activity, but if there is a group involved, children will also be working on their social skills.

Variations

- Instead of just going over the hurdles, challenge children to go under them. You can then have the kids alternate over and under through a series of hurdles for a more challenging activity.

- Set up a hurdle course, and time the children as they take their turns. Record their times and then graph the information or see if they can beat their previous time.

- Going under the hurdles will be more exciting with a small blanket from your dramatic play area draped over the hurdle. You can also drape a blanket over a series of hurdles to form a tunnel.

9

ACTIVITIES—DRAMATIC PLAY

The props in this chapter are great tools for extending and enriching dramatic play. These simple materials can be easily incorporated into your play area and will help children expand their pretend play repertoire. This is important, because the more time children spend engaged in meaty dramatic play, the more chances they will have to develop important social skills, try on new personas, deepen language skills, and build relationships.

The dramatic play area is a safe haven for young children to learn about how the world works. They can practice being parents, puppies, pirates, postal workers, pediatricians, penguins, or plumbers. They can construct complex and new social situations or reenact recent episodes from their own lives (which are often just as complex and new). They can practice being the people they may one day become, interacting with people they may perhaps meet, and living situations they probably will experience.

Dramatic play time is a powerful learning opportunity. These props, and plenty of time to use them, can help enrich this area of your program and offer children new imaginary roads to travel as they prepare for their future real lives.

Play Expanding Pipe

This is one of those things you just place in front of the kids and wait for them to use it. We had a few sections of drain tile, a flexible plastic pipe used for drainage, left over from a project at our house and decided to just toss them into the play area and see what the kids did with them. They played. They poured sand through them. They imagined they were giant snakes or dragons. They toted them around with no apparent direction or destination. This is just a nice, simple, and weatherproof play prop for your outside play area.

Ages
12 mos.
and up

Materials

☐ 10-foot section of 4-inch drain tile

Tools

☐ Utility knife

Estimated Build Cost

A 10-foot section will cost about $3, and 100 feet will cost around $25.

Directions

1. Cut your newly acquired drain tile into 2-foot to 4-foot sections with a sharp utility knife.

2. Place in a pile in your outside play area.

3. Watch as the children discover the materials and begin to integrate them into their play.

Storage

This pipe is weatherproof, so you can leave it on your play area all year long.

What's Learned

The learning will depend on how the children choose to interact with the materials. They will probably integrate the drain tile into their dramatic and physical play in a variety of ways. This will work social, motor, cognitive, and language skills.

Variations

- It's fun to talk through long sections of the drain tile. Consider keeping a long section around as an outside telephone.

- The sections are great for sand and water play.

- The sections are big but not heavy. Small children will feel very powerful when they find they can easily lift and tote around what they see as giant pieces of pipe.

- Children can send small cars, balls, sticks, and other items racing down pipes set at an angle.

Turning On New Ideas

Need a switch to turn on your kitchen light when you come home from work? Need a way to start the engines in your spaceship so you can save the world? Need to control the robot you've just constructed? This easy project will meet those needs and more when you introduce it to your dramatic play area.

Ages
12 mos.
and up

Materials

☐ Plastic electrical box

☐ Light switch

Tools

☐ Screwdriver

Estimated Build Cost

You'll spend around $2 on the materials for this project.

Directions

1. Construction of this project consists of installing the switch into the box. First, if the box you purchased has nails sticking out of its side, remove them.

2. Now all you have to do is screw the switch into the box. There will be two screws that align with mounting holes in the box. Tighten the screws and you're done.

3. You may be tempted to install a face plate over the switch to make it look pretty. We suggest that you do not. We tried a variety of switch plates while researching this project and found that the plastic ones will shatter if dropped, the wood ones splinter easily, and the metal ones have sharp edges that will easily cut a child. Leaving it without a cover is safest and easiest.

4. Now, all you have to do is leave the switch sitting in your dramatic play area. Someone will pick it up and start playing. Once they know it is there, this simple little item will be given many jobs during dramatic play.

Storage

These items will not take much room in a tote or on a shelf when not in use.

What's Learned

This prop is great for extending and enhancing dramatic play and all the wonderful learning that takes place during such play.

Variations

- Use double or triple boxes so you can have two or three switches in one unit.

- Mount a box or two on the wall or furniture in your dramatic play area.

- Use them for outside dramatic play too.

Dramatic Play via Special Delivery

The idea is simple: give kids somewhere to deliver mail and they will want to write letters. This activity is a great way to promote early literacy. Back in our child care center days, our preschool room had three mailboxes mounted throughout the space so children could create and deliver mail. This is an easy way to get kids involved in developing their reading and writing skills.

Ages
3
and up

TIP: This activity is appropriate for any child old enough to reach inside the mailbox.

Materials

☐ Mailbox

☐ Self-adhesive address numbers

☐ Envelopes

☐ Paper

☐ Pens, pencils, or crayons

Tools

☐ Two-sided mounting tape

Estimated Build Cost

Mailboxes cost from under $10 to over $100. Buy a cheap one.

Directions

1. All you really have to do is mount the mailbox someplace where the children have easy access. For smaller boxes, you can use heavy-duty two-sided mounting tape; it should easily support the box and all the mail the children will deliver. Larger boxes will require different mounting techniques. When it is mounted, you can affix your address numbers right to the mailbox.

2. Now make the envelopes, paper, and writing utensils available to the children. If they are interested, show them how to write the address on the letter so it corresponds to the mailbox. Explain that this is how the mail carrier knows where to bring letters. Encourage them to write and deliver letters. They will soon come to know quite a lot about mail and its delivery, and quickly incorporate this new knowledge into their dramatic play.

Storage

You should not need to store anything. If you want, you can keep a few pieces of paper and a pencil in the mailbox so the children can jot down quick notes whenever they feel the need.

What's Learned

The mailbox will invigorate children's interest in letters and words, reading and writing. They will eagerly pen missives to friends real and imagined. This is a simple and effective way to get them thinking about language. It is also a great dramatic play prop. A mysterious letter in the mail will open many fascinating imaginary worlds.

Variations

- Bring early language and literacy outside by mounting a mailbox in your outside play area.

- Invite your mail carrier over to visit. The kids will have tons of questions and love trying on the mailbag.

- Speaking of mailbags, make a kid-sized one for them to use.

- Help children who are developmentally ready to learn their home addresses (the age a child is ready for this can vary widely).

- How does the mail carrier know where to bring all those letters? Discuss maps.

What's That Dinging Sound?

Children love to play with doorbells, although adults are not always as fond of this type of play. Since kids like it so much, we decided to install a doorbell dedicated solely to child's play. Mobile infants and toddlers will love the power the button gives them, and older children will incorporate the bell into their dramatic play.

When we first installed a wireless doorbell in our playroom, one preschooler asked, "What's that dinging sound?" after he pushed the button he found mounted on the wall. He soon realized the button pushing was related to the dinging sound; he had taught himself about cause-and-effect relationships.

Ages
12 mos.
and up

TIP: Depending on the brand, the face plate of your button unit may pull off so the battery can be replaced. If it does, you will want to use a few pieces of Scotch tape to secure it in place. Curious toddlers will figure out how to pull it off if you don't.

Materials

☐ Wireless plug-in doorbell

☐ Duct tape

☐ Screws

Tools

☐ Screwdriver

Estimated Build Cost

We have seen wireless plug-in doorbells ranging in price from $8 to $50 or more. If you purchase one for play, purchase an inexpensive one. Ours has held up very well to daily use.

Directions

1. The doorbell you purchase should have two components: a button unit that you will attach someplace the kids can access it, and a bell unit that will plug into an electrical outlet. You do not want to purchase a doorbell that requires wiring.

2. To install, select an outlet in your play area and plug in the bell unit.

3. The next step is to mount the button unit. Choose a location that will allow children the best access. Mount this unit with a couple of screws. We tried two-sided mounting tape, but it was not strong enough to stand up to the persistence of toddlers who wanted to remove the button.

4. Test the button. You will probably discover that the sound is a bit loud and would drive you crazy after a few hours of constant ringing; apparently doorbells do not know how to use their inside voices. We made this discovery and quickly found a remedy to the problem—duct tape. The bell unit has an internal speaker and slots in its face for the sound to exit. Cover some of these slots with duct tape. You will have to experiment until you get a sound you can live with happily; too little hole coverage will drive you batty, but with too much you will not hear the bell at all. Test a few options and you will soon find the perfect inside-play doorbell sound.

5. Demonstrate the bell for the children if you want. We recommend letting them discover and test the button on their own. Remember, learning in young children is based on self-discovery and exploration.

Storage

Install it and forget about it. If you choose to take it out of your play rotation for a while, just unplug the bell unit and stick it in a drawer or closet until you want to use it again.

What's Learned

This is a great tool for teaching cause-and-effect relationships. Children will also love the power they have to make the bell ring whenever they want. This is a very empowering and gratifying piece of equipment for young children.

Variations

- Periodically move the bell unit to another location so the sound emanates from a different location.

- Most units have at least two ring settings allowing you to easily change the tone that is played when the button is pushed.

- Use the doorbell to signal pickup time or some other event in your program.

Cleaning Up in the Dramatic Play Area

This is one of the many projects in this book inspired, built, or improved by the children in our family child care program. It's a simple project inspired by something children see around their homes. We were really impressed when we first saw them build and use their own vacuum cleaners out of the PVC pipes from the Pipe Construction Set in chapter 15.

Ages
12 mos.
and up

Materials

☐ Pipe Construction Set (see page 184)

Tools

None

Estimated Build Cost

None

Directions

1. Construction is simple; connect the perpendicular hole of a tee-fitting to a long piece of pipe.

2. Place a 4-inch long piece of pipe in each of the other holes to form the vacuum's base.

3. On the other end of the long pipe, add a 45-degree elbow and a piece of 4-inch pipe to make a handle. You have created a silent, cordless, child-propelled vacuum cleaner!

Storage

Don't store it; just return the pipes to the Pipe Construction Set tote. The children can rebuild the next time you play.

What's Learned

While vacuuming, children are using their large- and small-muscle skills. Moving their arms and wrists will help develop the muscles and tendons used in writing. They will also probably be socializing with other children, discussing who has vacuumed what or who will tend to the babies who were awakened by the machine's noise. On top of that, you'll have a nice clean play area.

Variations

- You can make very long or very wide vacuums that will maneuver differently.

- You can encourage the kids to develop their own fancy versions.

- You can grab your duct tape, tape a flashlight to a few vacuums, and turn out the lights to simulate nocturnal vacuuming.

- With a few simple modifications, a boy in our program turned his vacuum into a motorcycle and sped off down the hall!

10

ACTIVITIES—NURTURING AND CARING

The great thing about working with young children is that if you lie down on the floor in the middle of the playroom, yawn, and close your eyes, some caring little person will probably bring you a blanket and pillow and offer to read you a story. If you pretend to cough, they will bring you a pretend bowl of soup. If you pretend to limp, they will wrap your broken leg in a cast made of doll blankets. If you look sad, they will want to find a way to comfort you. Caregiving is all about strong interpersonal relationships built on respect, empathy, and admiration. Time strengthens and galvanizes these relationships.

Children who are cared for in warm, nurturing, safe, loving, empathic environments generally internalize those traits. Caregiving is instinctual; but it takes practice. Whether children are playing veterinarian, feeding birds, or growing tomatoes, the activities in this chapter will help promote their nurturing and caring. These activities help lay a solid foundation that the children will build their personal relationships on for their entire lives. Interpersonal relationships are complicated dances; learning to nurture and care for others is not an easy task and requires lots of observation and practice. Make sure the children you care for have ample opportunities to learn the important dance steps of nurturing and caring.

Is There a Doctor Behind That Mask?

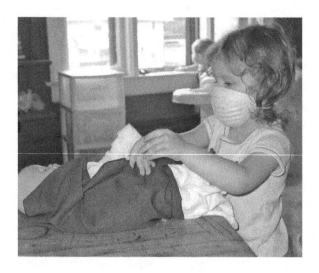

Making inexpensive dust masks available to children will instantly turn them into heart surgeons saving lives, veterinarians treating exotic animals, superheroes saving the world, and all kinds of other real and imagined people. On the other hand, you may just have a bunch of kids wearing masks as they paint, build with blocks, or read books. The novelty of this play prop is its biggest draw.

Ages
2
and up

Materials

☐ Dust masks

> **TIP:** This activity is appropriate for any child old enough to indicate that she wants one.

Tools

☐ Scissors

☐ Marker

Estimated Build Cost

A pack of five masks should cost around $2. They are even cheaper if you buy in bulk.

Directions

1. The only real preparation is a bit of mask customization. Most masks come with a thin strip of metal that can be shaped to fit across the bridge of the wearer's nose. Remove it and throw it away. They generally are not attached securely, and you do not need little pieces of metal floating around a room full of children.

2. The other customization involves fitting the masks to the children's faces. Without this step, the masks will be uncomfortable and not much fun. You will probably need to trim the top and/or bottom of the mask to make it fit properly. Just grab your scissors and snip away some material until you get a good fit.

3. The other adjustment you may want to consider is to shorten the elastic cord so the mask will stay on a child's head. You can easily do this by tying a knot in the elastic cord.

4. We also recommend making a mask for every child and writing their names on them to reduce the spread of germs. A bunch of community masks anyone can use might be easier, but assigning masks to individuals is healthier and also helps them learn to recognize their names. For younger children, consider using stickers or just the first letter of their name.

Storage

Store your masks in a large freezer bag.

What's Learned

What they learn will depend wholly on where their imaginations take them. This play prop will induce and support dramatic play that is beneficial to children in a myriad of ways. This type of play helps children discover themselves and practice different personas and skills. While they play, you can discuss all the people who need to wear masks like these when they care for other living things.

Variations

- Use markers to draw new mouths and noses on the masks for specialized dramatic play. Turn the children into aliens or alligators.

- Discuss how their breath feels as they breathe with the masks on. Have them take a few moments to listen to and feel their breath as it moves in and out of their lungs.

- Discuss how the masks are made to help keep our lungs clean. Explain how the lungs provide our bodies with the oxygen we need to live.

- We have found that the children sometimes just enjoy wearing the masks as they go about their day. They seem to enjoy the novelty.

Bedtime for Baby

Every dramatic play area needs a baby bed! This project is something you can construct alone or with a small group of children (we recommend letting the kids help if you're up to the challenge). It will be a great addition to your dramatic play area and will give your baby dolls a place to rest after all the rocking, feeding, and changing they get.

Ages **18** mos. and up

Materials

☐ Pipe Construction Set (see page 184)

☐ Nylon twine

☐ Duct tape

☐ Cardboard box (a photocopy-paper box would work great)

Tools

☐ Scissors

Estimated Build Cost

None

TIP: If you want a longer-lasting version of this project, replace the cardboard box with a durable plastic tote and consider gluing the pipe pieces together.

Directions

This is one of the most complex projects to build in this entire book.

1. From your Pipe Construction Set select the following:

- Four tee-fittings
- Eight 90-degree elbows
- Two straight pipe connectors
- Four 4-inch pipes
- Four 12-inch pipes
- Eight 10-inch pipes

2. Select four 10-inch pipes and the two straight pipe connectors. Connect two 10-inch pipes together with a straight pipe connector to complete a long section. Repeat with the other pipes and connector. Set these pieces aside.

3. Select the four 12-inch pipes, the eight 90-degree elbows, and the four 4-inch pipes. Place an elbow on both ends of each 12-inch pipe so that the open ends of the elbows are facing the same direction. Set two of these completed sections aside. Insert a 4-inch section of pipe into the open end of each elbow in the remaining two sections.

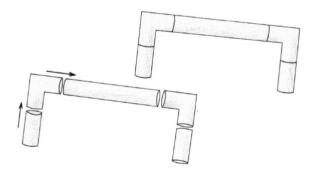

4. Select the four tee-fittings and the remaining four pieces of 10-inch pipe. Insert a piece of pipe into the perpendicular hole of each tee-fitting.

5. Select the two sections from step 2 and the tee-fittings from step 4. Add a tee-fitting to each end of the two straight sections so that the perpendicular holes are facing the same direction.

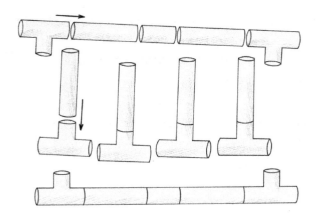

6. Select the two sections from the end of step 3 and the sections from step 5. Insert the ends of the 4-inch pipes into the open hole in the tee-fittings to create a rectangle. The perpendicular holes of the tee-fittings should face the ceiling.

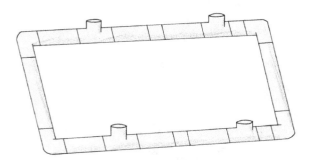

7. On each narrow end of the rectangle, connect the pipes protruding from the tee-fittings with the elbows of one of the remaining set-aside sections. You should have a long rectangle sitting on the floor with an upside-down U sticking up toward each end. Make sure all connections are solid. This is your completed base.

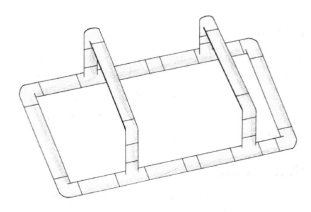

8. Use the scissors to punch a hole near each corner of the box along its narrow side.

9. Cut two sections of nylon twine about 24 inches long.

10. With one narrow end of the box facing you, thread a section of twine into the box and then out the other hole on that side. Even up the twine ends. Repeat for the other side.

11. On each side of the box, place a piece of duct tape over the twine between the holes.

12. Tie the twine ends from one side of the box near the elbows of one of the base uprights. Make sure you tie good knots. Repeat on the other end.

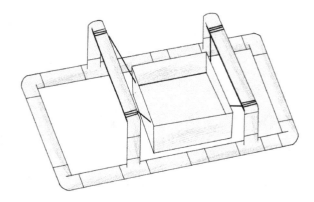

13. Insert baby doll and blankets.

14. Play.

Storage

No need to store it; when children have lost interest in the cradle as a play prop, just take it apart and return the PVC pieces to your building set. You can always rebuild the cradle in a few months when it will seem like something brand new.

What's Learned

Well, if you manage to build this project with the help of four or five preschoolers, you have learned patience and focus—good for you! Using the cradle you built, the kids will learn a lot about socializing with peers as well as nurturing and caring for others. They will also develop language skills, problem solving, and all the other wonderful skills research shows come from dramatic play.

Variations

- Customize and modify this project as you see fit. We tried out lots of designs and this one was, believe it or not, the easiest to explain and the most durable.

- With this project complete you may want to challenge the kids, or yourself, to build other things for the baby dolls—maybe a high chair, changing table, or swing.

This Project Is for the Birds

If you do not already have a bird feeder that the children can observe and help tend, we recommend that you set one up soon. Watching birds congregate at a feeder is a great way for young children to learn about nature and develop an awareness of the natural world.

Ages
12 mos.
and up

Materials

☐ Bird feeder

☐ Bird food

Tools

None

Estimated Build Cost

Bird feeders range greatly in price, but you should be able to pick up a decent one for under $10, and there are all kinds of plans on the Internet to make them from recycled materials. Seed will cost around $10 for a 25-pound bag.

Directions

1. Select a location for your feeder. Ideally, you should select a site that the children can observe from a window while they are inside as well as while they are outside playing. Your feeder site should also be easy to get to for refilling and provide some protection for the birds while feeding.

They need a clear field of view to keep an eye out for predators and a place to retreat to if they spot danger.

2. Hang and fill your feeder. Try to make the children a part of the bird-feeding process. They can help hang the feeder as well as maintain it throughout the year. Spend time with them watching the birds come and go. It may take a while to attract birds, and you have to maintain a steady food supply to keep them coming back.

Storage

Store your seed in a cool, dry location that you can easily access when needed.

What's Learned

Children will develop observational skills while watching birds feed. The detail of the bird's plumage, their calls and songs, and the idiosyncratic actions of different species will give children much to watch. Children will observe all these things. They will also learn responsibility and dependability as they learn to tend the feeder, making sure it is always clean and full of food. The appreciation they develop for other living things is possibly the greatest thing they will learn from this project. The ability to appreciate the world around them and the creatures that share it is a wonderful thing.

Variations

- Add a bird bath. Children will delight in seeing the birds drink and splash in the water.

- Encourage children to count the birds at the feeder.

- Learn to identify the different birds that visit your feeder and recognize their songs.

Growing Seeds

Spending time nurturing a seed into a seedling is a great way to teach young children responsibility as they learn a bit about the science of life. The will enjoy the hands-on work of planting and caring for their seeds.

Ages
3
and up

Materials

☐ Bean seeds

☐ Water

☐ Paper towels

☐ Large-mouth clear plastic container

Tools

None

Estimated Build Cost

You probably have everything but the seeds lying around the house, and the seeds will cost you less than $2.

Directions

1. Start by crumpling three to five paper towels and placing them in the bottom of an empty clear plastic container; an applesauce jar works perfectly.

2. Next add water until the paper towels are moist.

3. Now drop in a few seeds, cover them with one more moist paper towel, and place the container in a sunny window.

4. Check it every day with the children and add water as needed. You want it to be moist, but not too wet. The advantage to this method is that you can see the seed the whole time and do not have to wonder what is going on below the surface. Discuss the changes you see with the children each time you check the seeds. It will take a while, but you will soon see the seed sprout and grow.

5. Let this project grow if the children show an interest. If the children are still interested in the process of seeds growing into plants, consider purchasing some flower or vegetable seeds that you can grow and tend in the ground or in a container. The staff working in your local home center's lawn and garden department will be able to suggest some hardy plants and provide all the advice you need.

Storage

There should be nothing to store.

What's Learned

Most important, children learn to be caretakers and nurturers during this activity. They learn to make observations and provide the appropriate care based on those observations. Their observation skills will also be honed while they watch their seeds develop. If you use the variations that concern measurement, graphing, and prediction, children will be learning math and science skills as well.

Variations

■ Read books about seeds.

■ Plant seeds that grow into something you can eat.

■ Encourage children to draw pictures of their seeds and the seedlings as they emerge.

- Measure the seeds and the different parts of the plants as they emerge: roots, stems, leaves.

- Graph the changes in the plant's growth over time.

- Have children predict what will happen next with their seedlings and then check their predictions against what really happens.

Caring for Plants

The last activity looked at seed-to-plant growth. This one focuses on long-term care of plants. House plant, flower bed, or vegetable garden, children should have the opportunity to take responsibility for the care and growth of a plant. This is an easy way for children to learn to care for another living thing and develop the skills needed to be responsible.

Ages
3
and up

TIP: Be prepared to give 3- and 4-year-olds help and support in caring for plants.

Materials

☐ Plant(s) of your choice

☐ Water

☐ Sunshine

Tools

None

Estimated Build Cost

Don't spend more than a few dollars per plant. You do not want to put a four-year-old in charge of caring for an expensive rare orchid.

Directions

1. Discuss types of plants with the children and visit your home center's plant nursery, if possible. Decide what plants you want to care for and make your purchase.

2. Plant and care for your plants as directed by their labeling. We suggest you build plant care into your daily or weekly schedule so that it becomes part of the routine. Children will be attentive caregivers to start with, but over time, their enthusiasm will flag. For this reason, it is a good idea to make the care routine habitual. You may want to create a chart that children can use to log their plant care activities.

3. Make plant observation part of the routine too. Are there new leaves, flowers, dying leaves, color changes, or bugs since you last visited your plant? Nurturing and observation skills need to be developed over time; help children care for the plants and notice small changes as time passes. This is also a great time to discuss how they themselves have changed over time. Ask if they remember when they couldn't walk, talk, or use the bathroom on their own. Discuss how people change and grow over time too.

Storage

Store any plant care supplies in an easy-to-access location.

What's Learned

Taking care of a plant will teach children to be responsible caregivers. It will teach them to be dependable, and it will be an empowering experience. They will understand that the well-being of that plant is their responsibility. This caregiving experience will also help children develop their observation skills. They will need to look for changes in their plant and make decisions about its care from those observations. They will also learn about cause-and-effect relationships; take care of a plant well and it will thrive, not so well and it will die.

Variations

- Visit a garden center to learn more about plants and plant care.

- Share children's literature and stories about plants.

- Let children draw pictures or write stories about their plants.

Baby Grass

This is a great sensory project. Children will enjoy observing and caring for the baby grass as it is planted, sprouts, and grows.

Ages
2
and up

Materials

☐ Shallow plastic container, no larger than 12 by 12 inches square

☐ Grass seed

☐ Paper towels

☐ Water

☐ Plastic freezer bag

TIP: Too much sun will kill your baby grass. It wants some sun, but a cool space with plenty of shade is the best place to let it grow.

Tools

None

Estimated Build Cost

You can purchase a pound of bulk grass seed for a few dollars, and you will need far less than a pound for this project.

Directions

1. Layer three or four paper towels in the bottom of your container; fold them to fit as needed.

2. Add water to the container to moisten the paper towels. You want them soaked, but you do not want lots of excess water.

3. Cover the surface of the paper towels with grass seed.

4. Place the container inside the plastic bag and seal the bag.

5. Place the container near a window where it will get a lot of light.

6. Check the seeds every day with the children. In a few days you will notice that the seeds are beginning to germinate. When this happens, unseal the bag so that the seedlings will get plenty of fresh air. As time goes by you will quickly have a thick layer of green grass. Keep the paper towels moist. The children will enjoy helping out by adding a bit of water or misting the grass with a spray bottle. Once most of the seeds have sprouted, you can remove the container from the bag. After removing the container from the bag, you will have to water the grass more often.

7. This is a sensory activity. Make sure you give children a chance to touch and smell the seeds before you plant; the moist paper towel before you add the seeds; the baby grass as it begins to sprout; the warm, humid interior of the plastic bag.

Encourage them to put words to what they see and smell if they are talkers.

Your grass will not last forever in this container, and that's fine. Keep checking it as it begins to die. Note the changes and discuss them with the children.

Storage

There should not be anything to store after the grass goes to the big compost bin in the sky (or your yard).

What's Learned

This activity is all about the senses. Children will learn a lot as they see, feel, and smell the seeds sprout, grow, and die. They can also pick up some basic science as you discuss the growing process, what plants need to live, and other related topics.

Variations

- Allow the children to use scissors to give the grass a "haircut" when it gets long.

- Have older children record what they observe in a journal. How many days did it take to germinate? What did the grass smell like? How many days did it take for the grass to get three inches long?

- Plant two other trays of seeds at the same time; keep one in a dark closet or cupboard and do not give the other any water. Have children observe how these different conditions affect the growth of the seeds.

11

ACTIVITIES—SENSORY PLAY

As an adult, you can probably imagine clearly the texture of sandpaper, the humid and earthy scent of mud, the sound of long fingernails on a chalkboard, the tug of two magnets as they draw together, and the shocking shivers produced by a cold splash of water on a hot day. These sensations are wholly new to young children who have not had the sensory experiences necessary to bring them to mind; you cannot fully imagine the spinal quiver induced by fingernails on a chalkboard until you have actually experienced fingernails on a chalkboard.

This chapter's activities will give children a chance to explore with their senses. Aside from the knowledge of the world they will glean from this sensory play (mud is messy, water is wet), they will tune their senses, develop fine-muscle skills, learn about cause-and-effect relationships, acquire new language, and reap other benefits.

One thing to remember is that not all children respond the same to sensory play. Some do not want to get wet or messy; others have very sensitive skin, eyes, and hearing. One extremely curious and adventurous child in our program is very sensitive to loud noises and can play in the mud for thirty minutes without getting dirty. Some people were unfazed by the above mention of fingernails and chalkboards; others are still lying on the floor quivering. Make sure you take the temperament of the children into consideration when playing, exploring, and discovering, and make adjustments as needed.

A Touchy Situation

The paint and decorating department of your local home center offers many materials that have interesting and distinctive textures. We will use some of these materials to stock a tactile sensory set for use with young children.

Ages
12 mos.
and under

Materials

☐ Sponges

☐ Sandpaper, different grits

☐ Foam paintbrushes

☐ Bristle paintbrushes

☐ Foam sanding blocks

☐ Abrasive pads

☐ Carpet samples

☐ Wallpaper samples

☐ Ceramic tile

☐ Tape

☐ Paint stirring sticks

☐ Flooring sample

☐ Ceiling tile sample

☐ Canvas drop cloth, small section

☐ Paint roller heads, small

Tools

None

Estimated Build Cost

You could spend a lot purchasing all these items at once. Consider borrowing materials from other projects in this chapter or adding to your tactile sensory set a little at a time.

Directions

1. There is not a lot of prep work for this activity. Simply collect some of the materials listed above and stick them in a tote. This activity is best with one or two small children when you have time for a small group experience.

2. Get down on the floor with the materials and the kids and let them explore. Talk about how the different textures feel. The children will not only be experiencing the texture of the materials, they will be listening to you describe them. This is a wonderful language experience. It is a chance for you to expand their growing vocabularies.

3. Younger children will try to use their mouths to explore the items. Don't discourage this learning scheme; it is a natural and normal activity for very young children.

Storage

These items, like so many others, store well in a gallon-size freezer bag.

What's Learned

The children will learn the textures of different materials and the rich vocabulary that comes along with the sensory experience. This is a great way to promote the integration of tactile sensory input and small-motor skills. Adults' hands have experienced a lot of different sensations; they have been there and touched that. The hands of children are different: they find new textures amazing and fresh. This looks like a simple little activity, but it really gives small children a vast amount of sensory input that helps them understand what the world is made of a bit better.

Variations

- Add a twist by blindfolding older children who are familiar with the items and asking them to identify them by touch.

- Add a new sensory experience: integrate the items into your water play. Most of the items will stand up to a little water play quite nicely.

- Encourage children to use their feet, cheeks, and other body parts to feel the materials.

Give Them a Hand with Their Painting

Rubber gloves make great disposable paint applicators and add a new twist to painting projects. Children will enjoy dabbing paint to make interesting textures and patterns and will find this painting variation fun and engaging.

Ages
12 mos.
and up

TIP: Keep an empty sack handy so the children can easily dispose of their applicators after use. This will help avoid a big paint mess.

Materials

☐ Rubber gloves

☐ Cable ties

☐ Paper

☐ Paint

☐ Clean-up supplies

Tools

☐ Scissors

Estimated Build Cost

You can purchase a few dozen gloves for a couple of dollars.

Directions

1. Start out with two rubber gloves held with the fingers facing down. Now fold the gloves in half.

2. With the fingers still facing down, secure a cable tie around the gloves about an inch below the fold.

3. Next cut off the excess from the cable tie. The area above the cable tie forms the handle and the area below is the applicator. You can fold, bend, and twist the gloves in all kinds of ways to make these applicators. Use your imagination and try some variations.

4. We suggest that you apply small globs of a few different paint colors to each child's paper and then show them how to dab, bounce, and hop their applicators through the paint. They will catch on soon and enjoy the activity.

Storage

Dispose of the used rubber-glove paintbrushes and store the unused ones in a large freezer bag.

What's Learned

This is a handy project for promoting a different range of wrist motion than painting usually provides. Painting with these applicators encourages small children to use their developing muscles in a different way and promotes better control over those muscles. This is also a way to encourage children to take new creative steps; the new painting tools will help inspire new artistic expressions.

Variations

- Stuff the glove fingers with tissue to fill them out; this will make a different impression on the paper.

- Challenge children to paint with their non-dominant hand.

- Make some small cuts in the rubber-glove paint applicator to give it a different texture.

- Partially inflate a rubber glove and tie it off to retain the air; it will look like a balloon with fingers. This version will make some unique patterns when dabbed into the paint.

Playing in the Mud

Kids need to play in the mud, and too many adults are reluctant to let them because of the resulting mess. This is a way to make the cleanest mud you've ever used. Don't get us wrong, this is still real mud, but since we're using potting soil it's clean mud. Children will love to squish their fingers in the nice cool glop on a warm spring morning, and you will love the fact that you do not have to dig a hole in your yard to procure the ingredients.

Ages
12 mos.
and up

TIP: Think about cleanup ahead of time so you are not stuck with a bunch of dirty hands and no plan after the activity is complete.

Materials

☐ Sterilized potting soil

☐ Water

☐ Shallow plastic tote

Tools

None

Estimated Build Cost

You can usually purchase a small bag of potting soil for under $3 and a large one for under $8.

Directions

1. The only preparatory task for this project is mixing the mud. We tried a few different potting soil mixes and discovered that we obtained a nice and slimy, but not overly wet, mud by mixing two parts water to five parts soil.

2. You can mix the two ingredients in your tote beforehand or have the children do the mixing as part of the activity. A small tote will accommodate two playing hands, and a large tote will allow four little hands to play together. Make sure all hands know they are supposed to keep the mud where it belongs or they will not be able to play. It is a good idea to provide enough space to make mud pies, cookies, and other yummy treats. This is an activity you might want to do outside.

Storage

Most potting soils come in resealable bags for easy storage. You can store your mud in the tote with the lid on for a day or two. Allow the mud to dry out before long-term storage in the tote.

What's Learned

Children will use all their senses while playing with the mud. They will enjoy the earthy smell, the squashy texture, the dark color, the squishy sounds, and maybe even the fresh dirt taste. This activity also encourages use of small-muscle skills and creativity as children form the mud into balls and other shapes.

Variations

- Let children play with the dry potting soil before you add the water.

- Experiment with different water-to-soil ratios to create different textures.

- Add some sand to the mix for a different texture.

- Instead of water, add ice to the soil on a hot summer day.

- Introduce some cars or other small manipulatives.

- Provide some containers or cookie sheets so children can make cakes and cookies.

Feeling the Alphabet

Children learn in a variety of ways; this project will help children who are tactile learners master their letters and numbers.

Ages
2
and up

Materials

☐ Sandpaper, 80 or 100 grit

☐ Spray adhesive

☐ Letter and number stencils, 2 to 4 inches tall

☐ Stiff cardboard or index cards

Tools

☐ Scissors

Estimated Build Cost

This project should cost less than $15, depending on the size of letters you make.

Directions

1. Start out by adhering the sandpaper to the stiff cardboard using the adhesive spray. Use cheap sandpaper with paper backing—no need to buy the good stuff for this project.

2. The next step is to trace and cut out letters and numbers. An alternative is to cut the letters and numbers from the sandpaper and then adhere them to index cards. This will give you some negative space behind the letters and make them more visible to some children.

3. One way to introduce the cards to the children is to sit with a small group and demonstrate how to trace the letters with a finger. The kids will need time to get to know these materials. They will want to hold, feel, and rub them on things. Make sure you allow time for this experience.

4. This is a prop that can be used in small groups as described above or in a one-on-one situation with a child who needs the attention. They are also great to add to your dramatic play area. Children will easily integrate the letters into their play.

Storage

Store this item in a plastic freezer bag.

What's Learned

This is a great sensory activity as well as a language and literacy project.

Variations

- Use many different grits of sandpaper for your letter set. This will allow a whole new dimension of learning. Now you can match and sort the letters based on their texture. You can also introduce concepts such as "rough," "rougher," and "roughest."

- Have older children complete this project and introduce it to younger kids.

- Think of other textures you could use for this project besides sandpaper.

Making Sandpaper Music

If you have a collection of those new plastic baby food containers and a burning desire to make some sandpaper music blocks, this is the project for you! We've been collecting those containers for a long time and this is a great way to put them to use. Kids will have lots of fun creating music, and these instruments are easy to build, store, and replace.

Materials

☐ Sandpaper, 80 or 100 grit

☐ Spray adhesive

☐ Plastic baby food containers

Tools

☐ Scissors

☐ Pen

Estimated Build Cost

A sheet of sandpaper will make more of these than you need. Figure a cost of $4 if you need to buy a whole pack of sandpaper.

Directions

1. Trace the bottom of a plastic baby food container onto a sheet of sandpaper and cut out the shape. Trace and cut out as many of these as you need to make your desired number of sandpaper music blocks.

2. Cover the bottom of the baby food containers and the back of the sandpaper cutouts with spray adhesive. Make sure you are in a well-ventilated area. Follow the directions on your spray can; for a stronger bond, most suggest waiting 60 seconds before adhering the surfaces.

3. Align and join the bottom of the baby food container to the back of the sandpaper. Press firmly to ensure full contact between the surfaces.

4. Introduce them to the children. They will love making different sounds with these easy-to-handle musical instruments.

Storage

Store this item in a plastic freezer bag.

What's Learned

This is a great sensory activity involving sound and touch. Children will learn about sound, texture, and rhythm while using the sandpaper blocks. Younger children will also learn about taste. We have met some toddlers who enjoy licking the sandpaper. The texture must be very interesting and unusual.

Variations

- Use different sandpaper grits.
- Put lids on the containers for a different sound.
- Try rubbing them on different surfaces.
- Discuss loud and soft sounds.
- Practice repeating different rhythms.

Feel the Force with Magnets

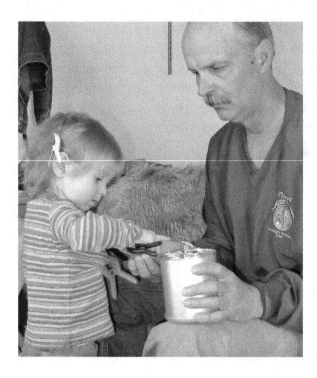

We wanted to find an easy way for small children to play with magnets without the risk of pinched fingers. It took a while, but we discovered this project, which is both easy and safe. Children will enjoy exploring and experimenting with the power of magnets.

Ages
12 mos.
and up

TIP: This activity is appropriate for children 3 years and up, with good supervision. Children 12 months to 3 years can also enjoy this activity but, because of choking hazards, should only use it one-on-one with an adult.

Materials

☐ 1- by 2-inch ceramic magnets, at least three. More is better.

☐ Empty powdered formula can and lid (the can must have a metal bottom)

☐ Paper clips—we favor the ones coated in colored plastic

Tools

None

Estimated Build Cost

Expect to spend between $5 and $10 on magnets and paper clips.

Directions

1. Place a number of magnets on the inside bottom of the can. The more magnets you use, the better. Three will work, but more will work better. The more magnets the stronger the magnetic pull with which to play and experiment.

2. Put the lid on the can and set it lid-side-down on a table. Dump the whole box of paper clips onto the metal can bottom and try to resist playing with them. It will be hard to do; the children will find the activity just as hard to resist. If you use enough magnets, you will find that the paper clips also stick to the can's sides.

Storage

For easy storage, keep your paper clips in the empty baby food container and keep that container

TIP: This project is best with one or two children at a time. Give them plenty of time to play and explore how the paper clips react to the magnets.

inside the formula can. The formula can will be easy to store on a shelf or in a tote.

What's Learned

When playing with the magnets and paper clips, children will begin to explore magnetic properties. The fact that they can place the paper clips on the can and invert it without the paper clips falling out will fascinate them, as will feeling the magnet draw a dangled clip toward its surface. The small-muscle work they do while manipulating the paper clips is also a benefit.

Variations

- Collect magnetic and nonmagnetic objects to make available for the children's experimentation.

- Instead of paper clips try a box of small bolts. The children can stand the bolts on end, stack them, and construct sculptures.

- Have two or three cans each with a different number of magnets inside. The children will discover that some cans are "stronger" than others are.

- Vary the number of magnets in the can each time you make it available to the children.

Feel the Outside When You're Inside

Earlier in this chapter we created a wonderfully fun manipulative by mixing potting soil and water. There are all kinds of other great items children can manipulate in the lawn and garden department. The texture, smell, weight, and sound of these items will stimulate children and pique their curiosity. This is a fantastic sensory activity that encourages play, exploration, and discovery.

Ages **12 mos.** and up

Materials

☐ Shallow tote

☐ Grass seed

☐ Bark mulch

☐ Stone mulch

☐ Peat moss

☐ Sand

☐ Landscaping bricks

Tools

None

Estimated Build Cost

$20 should buy all the items listed above, but that might give you more of everything than you need. We suggest you set small amounts of these items aside when you do your own lawn and garden work and let others know you are collecting landscape sensory items.

Directions

No special preparation is needed. Just add one of the above items to a tote and let the children play. They will love exploring the new materials.

Storage

Store individual items in large freezer bags and keep those bags in a tote.

What's Learned

Manipulating these items will engage children's senses. They will enjoy the different textures and smells as they play in the different matter. This is a great chance to experience and interact with new materials.

Variations

- Add water.

- Place the items in the freezer for an hour or two before play.

- Mix the items listed above to create new sensory experiences.

- Add the children's favorite small toys, cars, dinosaurs, or building blocks.

Splishing and Splashing in the Water....

The lawn and garden section of your favorite home center is full of different items that you can incorporate into water play with the children in your care. Since water play is so beneficial to young children, we suggest you find as many ways as possible to integrate it into your program.

Ages
12 mos.
and up

TIP: Be sure that this activity is well supervised. Prepare for cleanup before you start playing. Have towels and other supplies ready to go before the first splish or splash.

Materials

☐ Watering can

☐ Funnels

☐ Sprinklers

☐ Hoses

☐ Hose nozzles

☐ Spray bottles

Tools

None

Estimated Build Cost

Prices for these items vary greatly, but you do not have to purchase them all and you probably have some of them already.

Directions

1. Water play can, and should, take many forms. Running through a sprinkler, splashing in puddles, manipulating objects in a tote of shallow water, washing a car, playing catch with soggy sponges, toting a watering can from flower pot to flower pot—these are all ways children can actively engage in water play. Use the items listed above to facilitate water play with the children in your care. Vary the materials used to keep the activity fresh for the children, and make sure you give them the time they need to explore those materials.

2. Make sure you play safely. Children must always be well supervised; a child can quickly drown in a surprisingly small amount of water. Play safe.

Storage

Store materials in a garage or tote when not in use.

What's Learned

Lifting and toting water will promote large-muscle development. Pouring and dumping will promote small-motor development. This is also a sensory activity: children will see, hear, feel, taste, and smell the water as they play. Water play also promotes learning about cause-and-effect relationships and enhances observation skills.

Variations

- Many of the manipulatives in this book are safe to use in the water; try them out.
- Vary the temperature of the water for new sensations.
- Add soap to make bubbles.
- Empower children: trust them to control the hose and spray nozzle.
- Add food coloring and let children mix colors.

12

ACTIVITIES—CONSTRUCTION

> Very young children seem to have what could be called an Instinct of Workmanship. We tend not to see it, because they are unskillful and their materials crude. But watch the loving care with which a little child smoothes off a sand cake, or pats and shapes a mud pie. They want to make it as well as they can, not to please someone else but to satisfy themselves.
>
> —John Holt, *How Children Learn*

The projects in this chapter will allow children to use their Instinct of Workmanship to construct with a variety of materials. They will also provide the chance to satisfy their gnawing inner need to do a good job.

Young children are unskillful and their materials are crude, but their innate desire to do a good job is almost overpowering at times. Take the time to observe children at play or exploring new materials, see the concentration in their eyes, the focus on their faces. Look for the moment when a new idea clicks, the moment when they "get it." You will see their eyes brighten and their faces glow with pride. These moments of self-discovery are powerful and empowering. When working with young children, our goal should always be to create a safe, warm, and nurturing environment conducive to as many of these special moments as possible.

We have urged over and over throughout this book that children have the uninterrupted time they need for play, exploration, and discovery. We'll do it again. Since they are so unskilled, since they are new to almost everything they attempt, they need time for mastery, time to act on their Instinct of Workmanship. Give them that time.

Building Roads

This is a wonderful way to give children a place to drive their favorite little hot rod. Older children will enjoy laying out their own highways and byways, while younger kids will be happy to drive on pre-built roads.

Ages
18 mos.
and up

Materials

☐ Masking tape

Tools

None

Estimated Build Cost

A $2 roll of tape will allow you to construct this project many times.

Directions

1. Choosing a location for this activity is important. You want to provide as much space as possible for car traffic without interfering with other activities and the flow of human traffic. The more space the better, but if you have only a small area available, you can scale down the project.

2. What you want to do is lay out roads for your little truckers to travel. Think of the masking tape as the

> **TIP:** Lay out roadways under an area rug. Then you can roll up the rug when it is time for road play and easily cover it again when it is time for other activities.

curbs and the space between parallel tape strips as the roadbed. For little cars, we try to keep the curbs about 4 inches apart so traffic can easily flow in both directions. You will have to make adjustments for the vehicles that will use your roads. Just lay out the tape to form a variety of interconnected roads and intersections. You can create something formal with uniform city blocks or a whimsical knot of interrelated roadways. Have fun.

3. If you feel the children are developmentally ready, or just very eager to lay out their own roads, let them try. Tape is cheap and they will have a ton of fun even if they don't end up with drivable roads. Be available to help and supervise as needed. The construction process is a huge and important part of this activity for children ready to make the attempt. Give them ample time and only as much assistance as they need.

4. We have tried this project on a variety of floor surfaces and have had no problem getting the tape to stick or come off when we wanted. If you are concerned, consider using the blue painter's tape that is now readily available. It is more expensive, but it's less tacky and is designed for easy removal.

Storage

Store your tape collection in a gallon-size freezer bag.

What's Learned

The children who build their own roads are getting a good dose of self-empowerment and self-confidence from the project. They are learning that they are able, that they are creative, that they are powerful, and that they can be in control.

Being in control is a big part of the benefit for younger children too. Zooming around between the masking tape curbs looks like play, but these children are practicing to be adults. In their minds, they are potent adults in complete control of big and powerful machines.

Make this activity a frequent one. Young children need to experience power and control so that they will wield it wisely as adults.

Variations

- Add blocks so children can create buildings.

- Remove the ends from a few small boxes to create tunnels through which the cars can drive.

- Incorporate language and numbers by adding stop signs, other signage, and addresses to this play area.

Hook-and-Loop Domino Blocks

Self-adhesive hook-and-loop fasteners add a new dimension to building with blocks. Children will have fun exploring new ways to build with these customized blocks.

Ages
2
and up

Materials

☐ 25 Domino Blocks (see p. 194)

☐ 5-foot long roll of ¾-inch wide self-adhesive hook-and-loop fasteners

Tools

☐ Scissors

Estimated Build Cost

If you already have the blocks, this project will cost you only around $7 for the hook-and-loop fasteners.

Directions

1. First cut the 5-foot sections of hook-and-loop fasteners in half to create two sections of hook and two sections of loop 2½ feet long.

2. Now take one section of hooks and one of loops and cut them down the middle lengthwise to create pieces that are about ⅜ inch wide by 2½ feet long.

3. The next step is to attach the hook and loop to the blocks. The ⅜-inch-wide pieces are for the blocks' edges and the ¾-inch wide sections are for the blocks' faces. Cut smaller pieces about 1 inch long for the narrow edges and about 2 inches long for the long edges and faces. The only requirement is that each block have at least one hook and one loop. You can apply hook and loop to all six sides of a block or to any number of sides—it is up to you.

4. To play, just introduce the customized blocks to the children and let them explore. They will soon learn the properties of this new toy and build all sorts of interesting structures.

Storage

These blocks will easily store in a large freezer bag.

What's Learned

These blocks will allow children to explore a familiar toy in a new way. They will improve their hand-eye coordination and enhance their small-muscle skills through play with these blocks. The feel of the hook-and-loop fasteners will add to the learning by offering a unique tactile experience. This is also a great way for children to experiment with gravity and other physical science concepts.

Variations

- Drill a hole in one of the blocks and suspend it for some fun mid-air building.

- Stick a strip or two of hook-and-loop fastener on a wall or edge of a shelf so the kids can build in a different direction.

- Instead of hook-and-loop fasteners, use self-fastening magnet strips.

Do-It-Yourself Water Works

It just wouldn't be right if we had so many projects involving PVC pipe and didn't give kids a chance to get wet. This project will turn the kids into plumbers and give them a chance to get soaked. It is a perfect activity for a hot summer day. We suggest doing it outside.

Ages
12 mos.
and up

Materials

☐ Pipe Construction Set (see p. 184)

☐ Nylon twine

☐ Large funnel (you want the outlet's outside diameter to measure between ⅜ and ½ inch)

☐ Water

☐ Duct tape

☐ Plastic containers (cottage cheese, butter, etc.)

☐ Garden hose (optional)

TIP: Consider adding a few sections of clear PVC to your building set. Type "clear PVC pipe" into your favorite search engine and you should easily find a site that sells this material directly—you are unlikely to find it at your home center. Clear pipe will cost you between $1 and $2 a foot, about ten times the cost of the regular pipe. Fittings are even more expensive: clear 90-degree elbows cost around $5 each. The good news is that the clear pipe will work with the regular fittings. Investing $20 or $30 in some clear pipe adds a whole new dimension to this and other activities.

☐ Assorted ½-inch Schedule 40 PVC faucets and valves (optional)

Tools

- Scissors
- Cordless drill with ¼-inch bit

Estimated Build Cost

Faucets and valves run a few dollars each if you want to purchase them. You should have most of the other materials on hand.

Directions

1. To get started, insert the funnel into a piece of 4-inch pipe and secure it with duct tape. This will serve as the water inlet for your project.

2. To hang this structure, use the drill to make two holes (180 degrees from each other) in the rim of the funnel. Cut a 36-inch section of twine and securely tie one end to each of the holes you drilled in the funnel. Now find a safe location to hang the funnel. A site near a hose tap and away from any electricity is ideal. Hang the funnel at a height that will allow children to reach up and dump in water.

3. The next step is to lead the kids to the water; you won't have to make them play. Show them that water poured into the funnel will exit through the 4-inch pipe. Encourage them to add more pipes and fittings and see how the water moves through the system they build. The shallow plastic tote can be placed below the plumbing system as a target for the water.

4. Depending on your group size, you may want to hang additional funnels. With a very small group, the proper flooring, a plastic drop cloth, and a limited supply of water, this project can be done successfully inside.

Storage

No need for storage; just put the pipes back in their tote.

What's Learned

They will learn cause-and-effect relationships, fluid dynamics (how water acts), and logical thinking, along with the motor skills and social skills that come with such activities.

Variations

- Add some color. Challenge the children to build a system that will mix the water poured into two funnels. Then use food coloring and experiment with the color mixing machine.

- Try using warm water or ice water for a different experience.

- Hang your funnel over your sandbox for a wonderful sensory experience.

- Challenge the children to see how far uphill they can make water flow.

- Discuss with children how similar pipes help bring clean water to their homes and move soiled water away.

- Arrange a visit to a local plumbing shop or construction site to see how pipes are used in the "adult" world.

Build a Magical Mobile

If the kids think working with your Pipe Construction Set (chapter 15) is lots of fun on the floor, wait until they start building projects hanging in mid-air. Building with the pipes in this way engages the children's motor skills and imaginations in a completely new way. This project is so much fun you just might want to drill a hole in your playroom ceiling and install an eyebolt, if you haven't done so yet.

Ages
3
and up

TIP: If you haven't already installed a ¼-inch eyebolt in the ceiling of your playroom, it will come in handy for this and other projects. Make sure someone who knows what he or she is doing installs it and that it is securely attached to a ceiling beam.

Materials

☐ Pipe Construction Set (see p. 184)

☐ Nylon twine

☐ Medium safety pin

☐ Schedule 40 PVC four-way fitting

Tools

☐ Cordless drill and ¼-inch bit

Estimated Build Cost

None

Directions

1. Drill a hole through one side of the four-way PVC fitting. Then thread a piece of twine through the ¼-inch hole and out one of the fitting's openings. If you were unable to find a four-way fitting, any other connector will work for this project.

2. Securely tie the twine to the safety pin (if you do not have a safety pin, a small nut, washer, or even a paper clip will work). Pull the other end of the twine to draw the safety pin into the fitting.

3. The next step is to suspend the fitting. We recommend anchoring an eyebolt into your playroom ceiling. It will be great for this activity and has many other uses. After you install one you will wonder how life was possible without one. If you are unable, or unwilling, to put an eyebolt in your ceiling, you will need to find another suspension method. Tying it to a light fixture is a very bad idea;

TIP: Some kids will want to swing, or swing on, the suspended pipes. Others are going to want to whack at it like a piñata. Use your best judgment and think safety when dealing with these situations.

tying it to a sturdy tree branch arching over your outside play area is perfect.

4. You want the fitting to hang slightly above the heads of the children participating in this project. Make sure it is attached securely and then stick a few pipes and fittings into the suspended four-way connector.

5. At this point, the kids will be ready to take over; let them build.

Storage

No need for storage; just put the pipes back in their tote.

What's Learned

Children will use small-muscle skills making connections to the suspended structure. They will use large-motor skills while bending, twisting, and reaching over their heads. They will also experience how gravity wants to draw matter to the surface, how motion affects matter, and how cooperation with peers is often necessary to finish a job. Logical thinking and problem solving will also be huge parts of their play.

Variations

- Challenge children to keep all four sides in balance as they build.

- Decorate your mobile with yarn or paper streamers.

- Have children take turns adding pieces to a new structure or removing them from an existing structure.

Sponge Blocks

Sponges are a great way to reinvigorate block play in your program. They have a great texture, they are quiet, they are pliable, and they are fun. They add a kooky element to the block play area that will help reenergize play.

Ages 18 mos. and up

Materials

☐ Cellulose sponges

Tools

☐ Scissors

Estimated Build Cost

$2 should get you started; $10 will make a great block set.

Directions

1. First, you might not find sponges in the paint and decorating department. Sometimes they are there near the tape, drop cloths, and other painting supplies, but sometimes they are in the automotive department. No matter where you find them, they are worth the search.

2. We recommend cellulose sponges for this project; they are cheap and durable and have held up well in our program. You do not want the packages that come with two or three little sponges; you want the big pack of utility sponges. They usually come by the dozen. They are not the perfectly shaped sponges you get if you spend more money. These are the sponges that didn't make the cut; they are imperfect, but you can get twelve of them for less than $2. Besides, we are going to cut them up anyway.

3. To make your blocks, simply crack open a bag of these utility sponges and cut them into smaller pieces. We do not recommend anything smaller than 2 by 2 inches square and suggest you keep them much bigger for very young children.

4. Once you have them cut up, just dump them into your block area. We just put them out and built a few small towers. The children caught on quickly and loved them.

Storage

Store this item in a plastic freezer bag.

What's Learned

Tactile discrimination is the big focus of this project; the kids will learn the sensory differences between wet, moist, and dry sponges. They will fine-tune their sense of touch with this activity. They will also call their small-muscle skills into action while they are using their imaginations to build structures of all types.

Variations

- Try wetting the sponges before play.
- Wet and freeze a few sponges before giving them to the kids.
- Add them to your water play.
- For toddlers, try giving them a few wet sponges while they are sitting in a high chair. They will be easy to supervise and will love the activity.
- Add a few "special" sponges to the mix: different colors or materials or the ones with abrasive pads on one side. This will provide more visual and tactile stimulation.

- Use the sponge blocks with your other blocks and building materials.

- Add some sponges to your dramatic play area and let the kids decide how to use them.

Weatherproof Outside Building Blocks

We found that synthetic decking is a wonderful material for making outside building blocks. It does not splinter or decay and will stand up to all kinds of weather and use. Kids will enjoy toting and building with large pieces as much as they will enjoy sand or water play with smaller blocks. Like all blocks, these props are so versatile they are sure to be a favorite among the children.

Ages
12 mos.
and up

Materials

☐ Solid core synthetic decking

Tools

☐ Circular saw or power miter saw

Estimated Build Cost

An 8-foot section will cost around $12.

Directions

1. Just cut the big pieces of decking into smaller pieces. If you are uncomfortable with power tools, find someone willing and able to do the cutting. Different companies have their own recipes for making synthetic deck, but they all cut the same as wood. Large blocks will promote large-muscle activity; we cut a number of planks ranging in size from 2 to 4 feet in length. You may also choose to cut some smaller blocks for use in sand or water play. We do not recommend cutting them shorter than 6 inches long. Most of this decking comes in earth-tone colors, and shorter blocks will get lost in the yard easily. You do not want to run into one of these blocks with your lawn mower.

2. After you have cut the blocks, place them in a conspicuous place in your play area for the children to discover on their own. Make sure they know the blocks are there for them, and they will start exploring and playing with the materials.

Storage

Stack them in a corner of your outside play area when not in use. They will stand up to even the harshest weather.

What's Learned

These blocks are great for promoting large- and small-motor activity. They are also a great prop for inspiring creative play. Since children are used to block play as an indoor activity, the simple change in environment from indoor to outdoor will also help to stimulate their imaginations and encourage creative play.

Variations

- Challenge the children to build letters and numbers with the large blocks.

- Let the children use markers or paint to decorate the small blocks.

- Create obstacle courses with the large blocks and time the children as they take turns completing the course. You can also add another level of sophistication to the game by graphing their times.

13

ACTIVITIES—EXPLORING TOOLS

Most young children find themselves drawn to tools. They want to handle them and see how they work. Whether the tool is a hammer or a steamroller, they want to know more. Tools inspire all kinds of curiosity and questions. Why not? Tools are powerful. In children's eyes, tools allow big people to do big things: hang a picture, pave a road, build a bridge, plant a tree, unclog a drain, cut a board, or weave a blanket.

The activities in this chapter are empowering because they put real tools in the hands of children. This not only helps teach proper use and safety, but also gives them a chance to be the big dog, to be in control. Tastes of power and responsibility are important for young children. If we expect them to be responsible as adults, we need to give them chances to be responsible as children. Using tools is a great way for young children to practice being responsible and, in our experience, most children rise to the occasion. When given the chance, they will use hammers, saws, and other tools in a responsible manner. They want to be trusted, they want to be dependable, and they want to be powerful. These projects provide these opportunities.

Children will be using tools of one sort or another for their entire lives. These activities are a great way to help get them started.

Weaving Loom

This loom is a lot of fun, easy to build, and simple to store. It allows kids to express themselves as artists and craftspeople while working on skills that will help make them better readers, writers, and athletes.

Ages
2
and up

Materials

☐ Pipe Construction Set (see p. 184)

☐ Nylon twine

☐ Duct tape

☐ Pipe cleaners

Tools

☐ Scissors

Estimated Build Cost

None

Directions

1. Dig out the following pieces from your Pipe Construction Set:

- Two 90-degree elbows
- Four tee-fittings
- Six 4-inch pipes
- Two 15-inch pipes
- Two 12-inch pipes

2. Select two tee-fittings and stick a 4-inch pipe in each hole. These will serve as the loom's feet. Add a tee-fitting to the 4-inch pipe protruding from the perpendicular tee hole. Complete the base by connecting the feet together with a 15-inch pipe inserted into the perpendicular holes in the upper tee-fittings. Adjust the feet to stabilize the base.

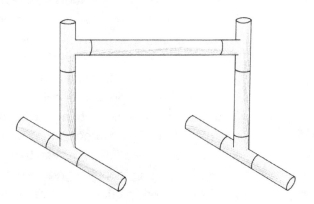

3. Insert a 12-inch pipe into the open tee-fitting hole on each side. Attach a 90-degree elbow to the remaining 15-inch pipe and install to form the loom top. This completes the frame.

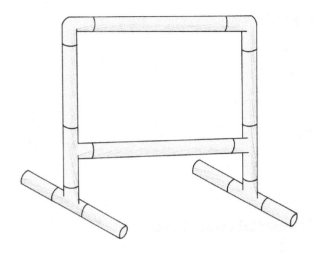

4. Now tie the end of your nylon twine roll to the lower-left corner of the rectangular pipe frame. To fill in the loom, wrap the twine from left to right around the pipes. Move up about an inch with each revolution, more for younger children, less for older. Tie the twine to the pipe when you reach the top.

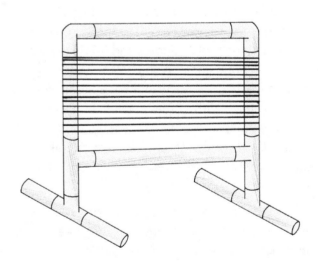

5. To complete construction, apply a piece of duct tape over the outside of each frame upright to cover

the twine as it wraps around the pipe. This will keep the twine from moving horizontally. You may also want to add a narrow piece of duct tape to the pipe visible between the twine. This will leave the vertical frame sections almost entirely covered in tape, but the twine will also be very stable.

6. To use, demonstrate how to weave a pipe cleaner vertically in and out between the horizontal twine. To make weaving easier for children who have problems, you may want to insert a white piece of cardboard, cut to the inner dimensions of the loom frame, between the two columns of twine. This will make the negative space more visible and improve the children's success.

Storage

If you rotate the feet 90 degrees, the whole unit should lie flat on a shelf for easy storage.

What's Learned

Children will develop their small-muscle skills and hand-eye coordination.

Variations

- Run the twine vertically instead of horizontally.
- Try weaving fabric, craft sticks, yarn, or other materials.
- Encourage more experienced weavers to create patterns.
- Use yarn instead of nylon twine in the steps above. Now let the kids weave with a different color of yarn. Make sure you press the rows together well, and when they are done you can cut their creation from the loom and display it.

Kid-Size Yard Tools

These tools are more maneuverable and manageable for small hands and muscles. Children will love to help do real work with these child-size versions of adult yard tools. Now is a great time to start building your collection of these useful tools.

Ages
3
and up

Materials

☐ Shovel

☐ Rake

☐ Hoe

Tools

☐ Saw

☐ Sandpaper

Estimated Build Cost

These yard tools can cost as little as $6 each if you look for deals.

Directions

1. Most of the children's yard tools we have seen are poorly made and not very durable. If you can find quality child-size yard tools, purchase them. An alternative is to customize the right adult tools for use by children. Look for tools with wooden handles, because customization requires shortening the tools' handles and this is easiest when they are made of wood. When shopping for a shovel to customize, look for a floral shovel. This is a spade with a smaller blade made for digging small plants or working in tight spaces. For a kids-size rake, look for an 8-inch shrub rake to customize. Any small hoe with a wooden handle will work.

2. You will want to cut between 18 and 30 inches off the end of the tool handle to make it easy for children to maneuver. When you have made your cut, use some sandpaper to smooth the cut surface.

3. Make these tools available to children during outside play and, if you garden, give them a chance to help. We recommend setting a small section of yard aside for them to dig. Make sure there are no underground utilities in this area and that their digging will not damage the roots of any trees or shrubs.

4. Be warned that a persistent child with a decent shovel can dig a pretty hefty hole. One summer our daughter, eight or nine years old at the time, dug a hole that was about 5 feet square and nearly 4 feet deep. It was a bigger hole than we expected, but not nearly as big as her prideful smile when she would show off her work to anyone who cared to look.

Storage

Store your yard tools in a dry location when not in use.

What's Learned

Working with real yard tools will teach children that they are capable of doing real adult work. Digging big holes and raking huge piles of leaves is hard work and a very empowering activity for children. These tools will also promote all kinds of good large-muscle activities and give a great cardio workout at the same time.

Variations

- Let the children plant and tend their own mini-garden.

- Look for children's books about gardening and yard tools.

- Let children use their tools to plant a new tree or shrub in your play area.

Measuring

Thermometers, rain gauges, and moisture meters are great tools for promoting an interest in science and the natural world. Children will like the hands-on use of these tools from the adult world.

Ages
3
and up

Materials

☐ Thermometer

☐ Rain gauge

☐ Moisture meter

☐ Paper

☐ Pencil or pen

Tools

None

Estimated Build Cost

You should be able to purchase all three of these instruments for under $20.

Directions

1. Each of these three instruments will come with its own directions for proper use. To use them with children, we suggest that you first introduce the children to the individual tools and explain what they are for: a thermometer measures temperature, a rain gauge measures precipitation, and a moisture meter measures soil moisture.

2. Allow the children to place the thermometer in different locations—the refrigerator, a sunny window—and see how the reading changes. Let them simulate rain with a spray bottle or watering can and see how the rain gauge fills. Permit them to test a number of locations in your yard with the moisture meter. Let them know the tools and understand their use.

3. Install the thermometer and rain gauge so you and the children can easily check them on a daily basis.

4. Once the children have some experience with these measuring tools, make a chart so you can record the information you collect with them. Use the headings Date, Noon Temperature, Precipitation, and Soil Moisture. Then help the children check the devices each day and record their readings.

Storage

The thermometer and rain gauge need no storage. Store the moisture meter according to the manufacturer's recommendations.

What's Learned

Children will learn to use these tools to make scientific observations about the world around them. This tool use is very empowering for children; they learn that they are powerful, capable, and authoritative.

Variations

- Record the children's readings once a week for a year and then figure out which week was the warmest, coldest, and wettest in your area.

- Check the TV or newspaper to see how the temperature and rainfall they report compares to your readings.

- Track the temperature hourly throughout the day and see how much it changed.

Kids' Tool Kit

A kid-size set of tools is a wonderful way to improve small-muscle skills and build confidence. The problem is that many adults are not very confident around tools and feel uncomfortable using them with children. This project may help build your confidence and tool know-how as well as the children's.

Ages
2
and up

Materials

- ☐ Toolbox
- ☐ Hammer
- ☐ Level
- ☐ Coping saw
- ☐ Clamps
- ☐ Brace
- ☐ Adjustable wrench
- ☐ Tape measure
- ☐ Screwdrivers, Phillips and flat-head
- ☐ Apron
- ☐ Safety goggles
- ☐ Gloves
- ☐ Pliers
- ☐ Carpenters' pencil
- ☐ Scrap wood, 1-by-2-inch to 1-by-6-inch pine boards up to 3 feet long

Tools

In this project, the materials and tools are the same thing.

Estimated Build Cost

You could easily spend over $50 on these tools. Start small, adding to your collection over time.

Directions

1. Don't rush out and buy everything on the list above, especially if you are not a confident tool user. Start with a toolbox and a few items you feel comfortable with from the list. Look for small tools that the children will be able to manipulate with ease. There should not be much problem finding all the items listed above in a child-friendly size.

2. Introduce the tools to the children after you have taken time to get to know them. Always act with safety in mind. Younger kids will be content to pretend to build and work using the real tools. Older kids will want to cut wood, screw in screws, and hammer nails. Do these things in well-supervised small groups.

3. As time passes, add items to your toolbox. The creation of your tool collection should be an ongoing project.

Storage

Your toolbox should store easily on a shelf when not in use.

What's Learned

Fine- and large-motor skills, hand-eye coordination, problem solving, logical thinking, and creative problem solving are just a few of the things kids will learn while working with tools.

The boost to their self-esteem and sense of self will be one of the biggest benefits you will see. It is empowering for children to be trusted to use such important tools from the adult world.

Variations

Take it from a family with more tools than are really needed (our daughter received her own cordless drill for Christmas when she was nine years old), the variety of tools you could share with children and the things you can do with them are endless.

Safe Sawing with Children

Slicing through a hunk of wood with a sharp piece of steel is a very empowering experience for a young child. If you choose the correct saw and the right wood and follow some safety precautions, this is a fun and safe activity. Children will love the power and control this activity provides.

Ages
3
and up

Materials

☐ 1-by-2-inch pine boards

☐ Safety goggles

Tools

☐ 15-inch long crosscut handsaw with 8 to 10 teeth per inch. Choose a saw with a firm blade. If you need help, ask a salesperson for a good saw for crosscutting wood with young children.

☐ Two clamps

Estimated Build Cost

Expect to pay between $10 and $20 for a good handsaw. You can purchase a pair of impact safety goggles for around $3, and clamps are a few dollars apiece if you need to buy them. Eight-foot 1-by-2-inch boards cost around $1 each.

Directions

1. First off, if you're not at ease using a handsaw, you need to spend some time practicing and improving your comfort level. Put on some safety goggles and cut off some 4-inch sections of a 1-by-2 so you are comfortable with the process. Here are some tips:

- Hold the board securely to a stable surface so that the location of your cut hangs over the edge. Clamps are a great way to keep the board in place.

- Mark a starting point on the opposite side of the board.

- Rest the saw at an angle on the mark you made so that most of the teeth are below the wood surface.

- Draw the saw toward you while pressing down firmly. Lift the saw and repeat the backward pull. Repeat until you create a notch where the starting mark was.

- Now you can continue sawing back and forth. As you reach the final few strokes, avoid using as much downward pressure to prevent splintering.

Demonstrate the above steps for the children after you have mastered them. Give each child a chance to hold the saw and lightly touch its teeth. They need to know this is a very sharp tool and that they must be very careful and cautious to avoid injury.

2. Every time a child cuts, there should be an adult closely supervising. Make sure the children know the saw is only for cutting the wood you give them to cut and that it is not to be waved around or mistreated in any way. You don't want to scare them, but you do need to make sure they are well informed about how to be safe with the tool.

3. When children cut, you may need to stand behind them and help guide the saw. Give the help they need but let them do as much as possible on their own. Keep the cut-off pieces short to prolong the life of your 1-by-2; 3 to 6 inches is a good range.

4. Make sure the child has properly fitted eye protection. This activity is great during outside play. The children can take turns cutting while the others play.

Storage

Wood should be stored in a dry location, as should your saw.

What's Learned

Sawing will work small- and large-muscle groups and it will help develop hand-eye coordination. The biggest benefit from this activity is the self-empowerment that will come from completing a cut. As we said before, slicing through wood with a steel blade is a very empowering activity for children. They will feel powerful and in control, which is a good feeling for children to experience.

Variations

- Get out the tape measure and square to measure and mark lines to cut. This is a wonderful time to talk about numbers and words like *length, width, measure,* and *dimensions.*

- Try wider boards for older children who have mastered cutting through 1-by-2s.

Fun with Plungers

Okay, when you think of versatile and fun learning toys, your mind probably does not automatically think "plunger," but maybe it should. There are many ways to integrate this suction-cup-on-a-stick into child's play. The children in our program had so much fun with this item the day we introduced it that at the end of the day they were asking if they could bring it to their houses for the night. You'll have so much fun you might want to buy two, one for the kids and one for you. Besides, our son, Tyler, had a play plunger when he was two and over twelve years later we have no negative impact from the plunger play to report.

Ages
18 mos.
and up

Materials

☐ Plunger, fresh from the store, for play only

Tools

☐ Marker

Estimated Build Cost

You can pick up a shiny new plunger to play with for less than $5.

Directions

1. There is nothing to construct or prepare. Just write in big letters across the plunger "FOR PLAY ONLY" and set it down somewhere for the children to find. They will probably explain to you that their dad or mom has one of these and start plunging away at the floor.

2. Soon they will discover that they can make the plunger stick to smooth surfaces and that they have to use a lot of force to make it release. They will also discover that it will not stick to porous surfaces no matter how much they try.

Hunter, three years old, and Jack, four years old, spent the good part of a morning sticking the plunger to different surfaces around our house. Their favorite was a smooth plaster wall. Repeatedly they attached the plunger and pulled until it released. To their delight, the plunger's release often made them fall backward onto the floor. They also discovered that they could open the refrigerator by attaching the plunger to its door and lift things like ice cream buckets and boxes if they attached the plunger correctly.

3. Let your children explore. They will discover things that the plunger can do and things to do with the plunger.

Storage

Plungers will not take up much room if the handle is unscrewed. You should be able to find room for it on a shelf or in a tote.

What's Learned

While sticking and unsticking the plunger, kids will learn lots about creating and using the power of a vacuum. They will also get a great large-muscle workout.

Variations

- Children will point the plunger to the ceiling and see what they can carry in the bowl that is created.

- Play off the idea above and create a relay race where they carry balls or water balloons in the plunger.

- They will discover all kinds of ways to use the plunger in their dramatic play.

- We've seen kids use the play plunger for a "shifter thing" when driving imaginary trucks.

- The play plunger makes a great post when you play ring toss.

- We've seen lots of kids use the plunger as a microphone.

The Long and Short of Measuring Tools

Integrating measuring tools into your program's play environment is a magnificent way to involve children with reading, numbers, and mathematical concepts. Children will love the chance to use real measuring devices from the adult world in their play.

Materials

☐ 6-, 12-, and 18-inch rulers

☐ Yardstick

☐ Speed square

☐ Square

☐ Calipers

☐ Tape measures

Tools

None

Estimated Build Cost

You could spend big bucks purchasing expensive measuring tools; you shouldn't do this. Keep an eye out for sales and always buy inexpensive items. The more expensive options are more accurate and durable, but you don't need accuracy for this

> **TIP:** Avoid metal tape measures wider than ¼ inch. The tape can easily cut a little finger when retracted. You should be able to find fabric or plastic versions that are much safer for small hands.

application. Besides, the cheap stuff should stand up to the kids well. You can start out by spending $10 to $20 and add more measurers if there is a need.

Directions

1. Once you've acquired a few measuring devices, spend some time with the kids talking about numbers and why people might need to measure things. Show them how to draw a straight line with a ruler or square. Make sure they understand that these are important tools and must be used appropriately; we do not shoot, hit, or kill monsters with tape measures at our house.

2. You may want to spend some group time together measuring things, or you may want to make the measuring tools available to the children in their dramatic play. Either way, make sure children have access to paper and pencils so that they can write down their measurements. Recording the information they collect is a vital part of the measuring process.

3. To add more authenticity to the process, consider using the oddly shaped carpenters' pencils available in all hardware departments. They are made so they don't roll; kids will love their uniqueness.

Storage

We have our measuring tools stored in a . . . you guessed it . . . gallon-size freezer bag.

What's Learned

Working with measuring tools will help children integrate numbers and mathematical concepts into their daily lives. It will also help them develop stronger language and literacy skills, encourage hand-eye coordination, and improve spatial relations.

Variations

- Challenge older children to calculate the dimensions of tables, rooms, or outside play areas.

- Chart the lengths of items around the play area.

- Discuss the concepts of big and small, long and short, etc.

- Encourage older children to build their own measuring devices from common materials and use them. ("This room is 50 red blocks long," or "Juan is 12 of Ginger's feet tall.")

Hammer Time

This is a great activity for empowering young children. What could make you feel more grown up and in control than driving a pointed piece of steel into a hunk of wood?

Ages
2
and up

TIP: Children 3 years and up will have the most success driving nails, but properly supervised 2-year-olds may also want to try.

TIP: Make sure girls have as many chances to hammer nails and use tools as boys do. It is great for their self-esteem. They need to feel powerful and in control, just like boys do. These activities are great for promoting "girl power."

Materials

☐ Large block of wood

☐ Roofing nails, galvanized, 2 inches long

☐ Safety goggles

Tools

☐ Hammer(s), preferably child-size

Estimated Build Cost

You can pick up a pair of small hammers and a 1-pound box of nails for under $15.

Directions

1. We recommend an 18- to 24-inch-tall, 12- to 24-inch-diameter hunk of tree trunk for your wood block. If you put out the word to parents, friends, and neighbors, someone will bring you one.

2. Set this piece of wood in a corner of your outside play area and then start a few nails and give a child a hammer. We prefer roofing nails because they have large, easy-to-see and easy-to-hit heads.

3. Make sure you explain that the hammer is only for hitting nails, and enforce this rule. The partially embedded galvanized nails will stand up to the weather, but the "fresh" nails and hammers belong inside when not in use. You will want to start a few new nails now and then, and you may need to flip your log when the surface becomes nail covered. Older kids may be able to handle starting their own nails, but keep an eye on loose nails to avoid choking and poking.

4. If you cannot find, or do not have room for, a large log, a 2-foot-long piece of 6-by-6-inch post will work well. Consider contacting contractors specializing in fences or decks to see if they will give you some pieces of scrap from a job. Pieces of wood this size could be used inside, but we recommend outside use so the whole neighborhood can enjoy the sounds of hammering.

Storage

Make sure your nails and hammer are stored in a dry location to avoid rusting. A toolbox or large freezer bag will work fine.

What's Learned

Participants will learn hand-eye coordination while they are taking part in this very empowering activity. This is a great way for children to work their arm muscles and strengthen their hand and wrist muscles, which will in turn help them with their small-muscle skills during activities such as writing and drawing.

The empowering action of driving a pointy piece of cold steel into a wedge of wood should not be underestimated either. This is a great way to show children that they are growing and able to do grown-up activities.

Variations

- Use nails with smaller heads.

- Count how many hits it takes to drive a nail.

- Challenge kids to drive nails with the hammer in their nondominant hand.

Help Kids Get Things Straight

Allowing children to play with levels is a very empowering activity. They feel entrusted with an important tool from the adult world. They will test and retest every surface they see to determine if it is level and plumb.

Ages
2
and up

Materials

☐ Small spirit levels

Tools

None

Estimated Build Cost

Small levels can be purchased for under $5 each.

Directions

1. There is really no preparation for this activity. Just spend some time showing children how the bubble in the spirit level moves as the level moves. Show them that a horizontal surface is level when the bubble centers itself between the lines on the tube. When held vertically on a wall, the surface is plumb when the other tube's bubble is centered.

2. With this little bit of knowledge they can set off to test everything from your tables to your refrigerator. Younger children will have fun and feel important just being trusted with an adult tool. They will move from place to place studying the bubble as they hold the level to different surfaces. Older children, who have observation skills that are better developed, will show more concern when they find a surface that is not quite level. Make the level available for the children to use as they see fit.

Storage

We store our level collection in a large freezer bag.

What's Learned

Playing with levels enhances children's observation skills and small-motor skills. They are watching that tiny bubble and trying to adjust the level to center the bubble. They will test every surface they come in contact with and determine if it is level and plumb. Children will also gain a sense of importance when entrusted with this important tool that adults use to make buildings and other structures. This feeling of empowerment is an important thing for small children to experience.

Variations

- Use your level while building with blocks.

- Make a list of surfaces in your play area and challenge older children to test to see if they are level. They can record their findings on your list to incorporate writing into the activity.

- See if older children can level unlevel surfaces.

- Levels are fun additions to your dramatic play area.

14

ACTIVITIES—ART

The materials in this chapter are great for expanding and enhancing children's art projects. These items will put a new spin on art projects and encourage creativity and exploration of the materials.

The key to success is ensuring that the kids have the freedom to express themselves and create their own unique works of art. Don't force them into replicating an idealized adult version of a project; let them speak with their own creative voice. Kids' art should be open ended, child directed, and fun.

Art projects are a great way to develop useful skills, but their biggest benefit might come from the emotional release that often accompanies a creative act. Painting, sculpting, drawing, and other expressive activities allow children to release stress and are cathartic ways of dealing with troubling situations. We have often seen stressed kids request to draw or paint as a way to center themselves, to get grounded.

Make sure you allow them the time they need to fully express themselves and experience the materials; it is good for their physical and emotional development.

Crafty Paper Ideas

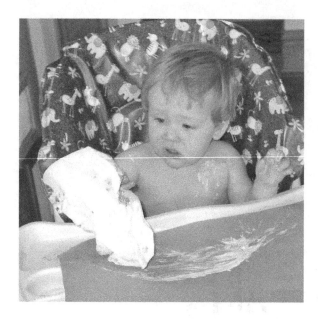

Masking paper is intended for use with masking tape to protect surfaces during painting and other finishing projects. It comes in rolls 100 to 200 feet long and widths of 4 to 12 inches. We have seen it in two colors: tan and green. Variety is supposed to be the spice of life, and this paper is a great way to spice up your arts and crafts projects.

Ages
2
and up

TIP: This activity is appropriate for all children old enough to show an interest in expressing themselves.

Materials

☐ Masking paper, a variety of widths

☐ Pens, pencils, markers, paint, or other medium

☐ Masking tape

Tools

☐ Scissors

Estimated Build Cost

Rolls of masking paper generally cost a few dollars each depending on their width.

Directions

1. The best part about this paper is that you can cut it to any length and let the children create. We often put down sheets that are over 6 feet long. Sometimes a group of children will work together on a large sheet of paper, and other times a single artist will create his own work.

2. The paper has a tendency to curl when it comes off the roll. We recommend taping the corners to the table with masking tape. This will also make creating easier for younger children; they can focus more on their project and less on keeping the paper still.

Storage

Put a rubber band around the roll to keep it from unfurling, and store with your other arts and crafts supplies.

What's Learned

Children will love the variety this type of paper offers, and it will stimulate their creativity. The paper will also play its part in the development of small-muscle skills and early literacy. Any time children write, draw, paint, or create using their hands, they are developing vital pre-literacy skills.

Variations

- Roll the paper out on the floor and let them lie on their bellies and write, paint, or draw.

- Infants and toddlers will love crumpling, shaking, and twisting large pieces of this paper. We have found it is pretty durable and will stand up well to this kind of exploratory play.

- The any-length-you-want sheets are also great for cutting, taping, and gluing.

- Because this paper is made to be moisture resistant, we have found that it's great for finger painting. The paint does not soak through as quickly as it does with other papers.

Wacky Paintbrushes

This is a very simple project that will add some variety to your arts and crafts activities. These customized paintbrushes will add a new twist to painting.

Materials

☐ A variety of cheap foam and bristle paintbrushes

Tools

☐ Scissors

Estimated Build Cost

This project should cost $10 or less, depending on how many brushes you purchase.

Directions

1. The only preparation this project requires is a little time with the scissors. What you want to do is cut a variety of angles, shapes, and patterns into the business end of the paintbrushes. Try to make each one unique.

2. When done, simply introduce them to the kids the next time you decide to paint.

Storage

Store your brushes in a gallon-size freezer bag.

What's Learned

Each brush will provide a different sensory experience. The children will have to hold the brushes in different ways and move them differently to make them "work." This is going to give their young wrists and fingers a good workout; great practice for holding a pencil when they start to write. This project will also give them all kinds of fun ways to express themselves in an artistic manner.

Variations

- Make some brushes available in your dramatic play area. The kids will quickly invent their own imaginary paint.

- Painting outside with water is lots of fun. The children in our program love to see the surface color change as they "paint" stone walls, sidewalks, and other objects.

- Show children how to gently "paint" the skin on their forearms or legs. This is a fun sensory activity.

Texture Paintings

Notched adhesive applicators are made for spreading adhesive for tiles and carpet. The notches help ensure that the bonding agent is properly applied for good adhesion. The small plastic applicators are inexpensive and meant to be disposable. We have found that they work well for texture painting. The notches leave swirls of parallel lines in the paint as children pull them across a piece of paper. These trowels are made with a variety of different notch shapes and depths.

Materials

☐ Plastic notched adhesive spreaders

☐ Paper (we recommend the masking paper described earlier in this chapter)

☐ Paint (your favorite finger paint, tempera, or washable paint)

Tools

None

> **TIP:** If you will not be able to clean the applicators right away, prepare a small container of warm soapy water before you paint. Then, after the project, the kids can drop their applicators in and you can just let them soak until you have time to clean.

Estimated Build Cost

We found a variety of styles all selling for around $1 each.

Directions

1. All you need to do is put globs of a few paint colors onto each child's paper and let them spread the colors. Children who are only used to painting with brushes will need some encouragement to give the new tools a chance, but most kids will jump right in and give it a try. This could (and should) get messy.

2. We recommend taping the corners of the paper so it does not slide around on the table. This will make the process easier for the children. You do not have to limit them to using the notched applicators; allow them to use brushes and their fingers if they wish.

3. When finished, make sure you clean the applicators thoroughly before the paint dries on them. It is a lot of work to clean dry paint out of all those little notches.

Storage

They easily store in a gallon-size freezer bag.

What's Learned

These applicators help develop the muscles needed for writing and are a great tool for artistic expression. Remember, the more, and more varied, experiences children have with art and the creative process the better. These activities build brain connections that are important for the development of complex thinking skills.

Variations

■ Use the applicators with playdough or clay.

■ Use the applicators during sand and water play.

Giant Paper Canvases

Sometimes children have ideas that are larger than a 12-by-18-inch piece of newsprint. This activity will allow them to express themselves on a grand scale. They will love the experience of creating their own "art" on a huge piece of paper.

Ages
2
and up

Materials

☐ Paper drop cloth

Tools

☐ Scissors

☐ Crayons

☐ Markers

☐ Paint (your favorite finger paint, tempera, or washable paint)

Estimated Build Cost

An 8-by-12-foot paper drop cloth will cost around $3.

Directions

1. Paper drop cloths usually measure about 8 by 12 feet and cost about $3; that is a big piece of paper. Unless you have lots of room to work, we recommend you cut one down into three or four smaller sections. This will make the paper more manageable and allow for more projects.

2. The simplest way to use this big paper is to place it on top of a table and let a group of kids start to work with paint, markers, or crayons. They will generally love not having to restrain themselves to a small piece of paper. Most kids like the opportunity to draw on a grand scale. We have, however, seen children almost unnerved by the experience at first. Such a large space to create in leaves them overwhelmed and wanting a smaller piece of paper for their project. They are usually soon comfortable with the new concept, but if they need a smaller piece of paper, give it to them.

3. Older children may enjoy having their own large section of paper to draw on or sharing one with a friend. They will probably want to come back to it over and over again until it is completed. With such a big work area, it is good to give them the time needed to complete the work.

Storage

Fold and store in a tote.

What's Learned

These large sections of paper are a great way to let young artists express themselves on a grand scale. This self-expression is important in developing self-esteem and creativity. The artistic process also promotes the small-muscle skills that are such an important component of writing. This project invites creativity, as do the following variations.

Variations

■ Trace the children's bodies and let them color and cut out their images.

■ Give infants and toddlers large sections of paper and allow them to explore the material with their hands, feet, and mouths.

■ Use as a tablecloth or drop cloth during messy arts and crafts projects.

■ Drape over a table to create a cozy kid-size clubhouse.

- Use it to create murals and banners for your dramatic play area or special events.

- Let them paint with their feet.

- Give them some scissors and let them practice their cutting skills.

- How about cutting giant snowflakes or paper dolls?

- Giant paper airplanes, anyone?

Scrap Wood Sculptures

If you were brave enough to put a saw in the hands of small children a few projects back, you have probably amassed a collection of wood scraps. This project will give you a creative way to use those scraps. Children will really enjoy building and decorating sculptures with the pieces they have cut.

Ages
2
and up

Materials

☐ Wood scraps

☐ Glue

☐ Paint, crayons, and/or markers

☐ Newspaper

Tools

☐ Sandpaper, 100 grit

Estimated Build Cost

You should have all these materials around from previous projects. If you need more wood scraps than you can generate, put the word out. Someone will put you in touch with a woodworker willing to share his or her scraps.

Directions

1. To avoid slivers, the first thing to do is lightly sand all the wood scraps. You do not need to make them smooth; you just want to soften all the edges a bit to avoid splintering. You can do this yourself ahead of time or let the children help with the sanding as part of the project.

2. This is a project that will take at least two days. On the first day let the children glue pieces of scrap wood into whatever arrangement they choose. Have them build their sculptures on a few sheets of newspaper to avoid a glue mess on your table. Set the structures aside so the glue can fully dry.

3. The final step is to paint their work. They are the artists; let them choose the colors they want to use and their favorite brush. Give them the time they need to complete their work. Let them tell you when they have finished. If you prefer to decorate with markers or crayons, you may choose to decorate the pieces of wood before you glue them together. This might make the board surfaces easier to reach for some children.

Storage

There is no need to store the projects; display them for a while, and then send them home with their makers.

What's Learned

Children will learn to tap into their innate creativity with this project. This is a wonderfully empowering activity, especially if they cut some of the boards used in the project. This project also works their small-muscle skills and hand-eye coordination.

Variations

■ Add other media to the mix: ribbon, paper, cardboard, other recyclable materials, etc. This will add more dimension and creativity to the projects.

■ Challenge the young artists to create something specific like the first letter of their names or a horse.

- Instead of gluing the wood scraps together, try using tape. This will give the children a different small-muscle experience.

- Let the children work in groups of two or three. This is a good way to introduce cooperative learning.

- Ask children to name their sculptures. They can also write or dictate descriptions of their work.

Messy Fun with Cement

What could be more fun (or messy) than preschoolers and wet cement? You have to be brave to take on this project, but the look on the faces of parents when you tell them about the project will be worth any anxiety.

Let the visions of firefighters frantically jackhammering children from large cement blocks fade from your mind. This project doesn't call for much cement, just enough to have a great tactile experience and maybe sculpt a thingamajig.

Ages
3
and up

TIP: This is not a project to do in the dining room. Keep it outside.

TIP: Do not do this project on very hot or sunny days. The heat and sunlight will have a negative impact on the curing process.

Materials

☐ Ready-mix cement, sand, or mortar mix

☐ Water

☐ Wet rags

☐ Ice cream buckets

☐ Tarp or plastic sheeting

☐ Spray bottle full of water

☐ Craft sticks

Tools

None

Estimated Build Cost

A 60-pound bag of ready-mix cement costs around $3 and it will allow a lot of playing. You should have most of the other items on hand unless you need to eat a few gallons of ice cream.

Directions

1. Beforehand do the following:

■ Spread a drop cloth or plastic sheeting over your work area; things could get messy.

■ Have a bucket of warm water and some wet rags standing by.

■ You should have one ice cream bucket for each child; other similar-size disposable containers will work. Pour an inch or two of dry cement mix into each container.

■ Have a hose or large container of clean water available.

■ Slowly take a few deep breaths and think about all the fun you are about to have.

2. Now, it is time to bring on the children. Make sure they are dressed to get messy. Give each child one of the containers of cement mix you prepared. Then help them slowly add water as they stir the mixture with their hands. The key word is slowly. The more water the more chance there is of a mess. Have them add water and stir until their mix is the consistency of chocolate chip cookie dough.

3. When they achieve the right consistency, it is time to sculpt. Let them dump their mixture onto the surface to knead and shape as they see fit. Give the children craft sticks so they can work the wet cement's surface. If the mixture starts to dry out and get too crumbly, you may need to add a very small amount of water to their mix with the spray bottle. When they are finished, have them clean their hands with a wet rag.

4. The projects should be placed in a cool shady area to cure. Cover each project with a thoroughly wrung out wet rag. While the cement cures, we suggest you lightly spray it with water a few times a day for the next three or four days. Try to avoid handling the projects during this time. They will probably be dry to the touch in a few hours, but you want them to strengthen and cure for a few days before handling. Have the children check on their projects daily and help with the misting.

Storage

Keep any unused cement mix in a very dry location for future use.

What's Learned

The gritty wetness of fresh cement is a wonderful tactile experience by itself. Just squishing their hands in the stuff will be a new sensory event for many children. They will use their developing small-motor skills in the process.

This activity is also great as a creative outlet. They will sculpt something that will in a few short days become almost as hard as rock. That is empowering.

Variations

- Mix other items into the cement before you sculpt. Ribbon, twine, small stones, marbles, etc., will work well.

- Children can apply the above items to their finished projects before they dry by gently pressing them into the wet cement.

- Paint the finished projects.

- Encourage children to write or dictate stories about their projects to display with them.

- You can mix up small batches of very wet or very dry mix for the sensory experience. Children will enjoy touching the different mixtures.

- No reason to let your hands have all the fun. Squish wet cement between your toes!

15

ACTIVITIES—LEARNING EQUIPMENT TO BUILD

We could have found space in the previous chapters for these projects, but because they require a little more work to put together we decided to group them together. In this chapter, you do most of the work ahead of time to create a learning toy for children to use. Some of the equipment you'll make in this chapter has already been referred to in other chapters, notably the Pipe Construction Set on the next page and the Domino Block Set on p. 194.

We wanted to save the tough stuff for last, but the tough stuff isn't all that complicated. These projects just have a few more steps or require power tools with which most people might not have experience. Don't be afraid. This whole book has been about giving children the chance to take on new challenges and develop new skills. Now it is your turn. We wouldn't have put anything into this book that we didn't think you could do. Trust us and try these projects out.

Pipe Construction Set

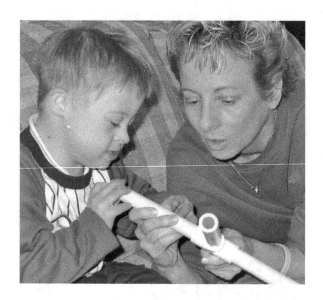

Children will love to construct all kinds of props and structures with this building set consisting of straight sections of PVC pipe and a variety of related fittings. The pieces of this basic building set can be used to construct many of the activities outlined in this chapter and will provide hours of fun and learning. The easiest way to introduce this project is to simply place it on the floor in front of a small group of children and step back. They will instinctively begin exploring the properties of the materials. They will start manipulating them, blowing into them, and building shapes almost automatically. All children between one year old and ten years old we have shared this play set with were drawn to the materials.

Ages
12 mos.
and up

Materials

☐ Four 10-foot pieces of ½-inch Schedule 40 PVC pipe

☐ Ten ½-inch Schedule 40 PVC 90-degree elbows

☐ Ten ½-inch Schedule 40 PVC 45-degree elbows

☐ Ten ½-inch Schedule 40 PVC connectors

☐ Ten ½-inch Schedule 40 PVC end caps

☐ Ten ½-inch Schedule 40 PVC tee-fittings

☐ Ten Schedule 40 PVC four-way fittings

Tools

☐ Tape measure

☐ Marker

☐ PVC pipe cutter or hacksaw. We recommend the pipe cutter for smooth cuts, but a hacksaw will work in a pinch. You should be able to purchase a pipe cutter for between $10 and $20.

Estimated Build Cost

You can purchase materials for a basic building set for around $30.

> **TIP:** If you are unfamiliar with items mentioned in this book, bring it along when shopping so you can point out to store staff exactly what you need.
>
> Schedule 40 PVC is the fancy name for this type of pipe. What you want to look for when shopping is white plastic pipe and fittings. The pipe will be marked with its size and Schedule 40 PVC. Stores usually group the fittings in the same aisle of the plumbing department.

Directions

1. The long pieces of pipe will probably be a bit dusty from shipping; it is easiest to wipe them down with a wet rag before cutting them.

2. To build this play set, simply measure and cut the 10-foot sections of pipe into smaller pieces:

- Cut the first section into thirty 4-inch pieces.
- Cut the second section into twenty 6-inch pieces.
- Cut the third section into twelve 10-inch pieces.
- Cut the last section into eight 15-inch pieces.

This will give you a very versatile beginner's set. You can add more pipes of different lengths as you see fit. We recommend that you do not make pieces shorter than 4 inches long to prevent choking. Children are also more likely to swing and hit with pieces longer than 15 inches.

3. If you use a PVC pipe cutter, you will end up with very smooth ends and there will be no need for sanding. If you use a hacksaw, you will probably need to go over the ends of each piece with 120-grit sandpaper to make them smooth.

4. Now mix the straight sections of pipe with the assorted fittings and start to play. The kids will eagerly begin to explore the materials, integrate them into their play, and discover all kinds of things to do with them.

Storage

We have found that a large shallow plastic tote is an ideal storage option for our Pipe Construction Set.

What's Learned

Small-muscle skills, large-motor skills, cognitive skills, and social skills are a few of the many things children will develop playing with PVC pipes. This building set is also wonderful for turning on a child's imagination.

Variations

- Purchase ½-inch PVC faucets and valves (usually around $2 each) to add some variety to this set.
- Depending on the ages of the children playing, you might also want to add masking tape, cardboard, nylon twine, funnels, tape measures, wooden blocks, and other activity expanders to the play area.
- This building set is also a wonderful addition to the dramatic play area—children will use the pipes to build props needed in their play.

TIP: Kids, usually boys in our experience, are going to want to shoot and hit with pipe sections. Sadly, one of the first things many kids want to construct is a weapon. Deal with this quickly and according to your program's policies. In our house, we do not shoot or hit so when pipes are used to violate this rule, the pipes are put away.

Fancy Fluttering Streamers

These easy-to-make props will really get kids up and moving. They will love making the colorful streamers fly, flutter, and flap through the air. The directions will explain how to make a set of six of these exciting, active play props.

Ages
2
and up

TIP: Remember that crossing over the midline of the body (an imaginary line running down a person's center) from one side to the other helps promote brain development. Encourage children to do this by asking if they can do things like touch the streamer to their opposite knee or shoulder.

Materials

☐ Two ⅜-inch dowels, 36 inches long

☐ Six number 3 ball bearing swivels with interlock snaps (you'll find these at your favorite fishing tackle store)

☐ Six small screw eyes

☐ Fluorescent flagging tape

Tools

☐ Scissors

☐ Saw

☐ Sandpaper, 120 grit

☐ Pliers

Estimated Build Cost

You can build six streamers for around $12. Not bad when similar items sell for $7 to $11 each in most early childhood equipment catalogs.

Directions

1. The first step is to cut each dowel into three sections, each 12 inches long.

2. After making the cuts, smooth the six pieces with 120-grit sandpaper.

3. Next install a screw eye into one end of each dowel section. You should be able to screw in the eyes without making a pilot hole. A pair of pliers may come in handy for the last few twists.

4. The ball bearing swivels have a closed ring on one end and a wire snap on the other end. Install a swivel onto each screw eye. Make sure to close the snap securely.

5. Now all you have to do is thread a piece of your flagging tape through the other end of the swivel. You might not think it will fit, but you'll be able to do it easily after the first one or two. Just pull the tape halfway through the eye. Friction will hold it in place, so there is no need for a knot. Size your flagging tape to the children who will use the streamers and the space in which they will be used. We recommend making them long and then shortening them if needed. If the tape wears out, it is very easy to replace.

6. To use, demonstrate to a group of children, and when they want to try (we promise they will) let them. Make sure you provide as much space as possible for ultimate enjoyment.

Storage

These streamers will fit perfectly into a large freezer bag.

What's Learned

This activity is wonderful for encouraging large-muscle movement when children run and jump with the ribbons. It also calls the small muscles of the wrist and hand into action when children twist and rotate the ribbon sticks. Another benefit is the freedom of self-expression that comes with their individual ribbon routines.

Variations

- Thread two different-colored tapes through each swivel for more colorful streamers.

- Use your streamers outside.

- Encourage children to use their streamers with their nondominant hand.

- Use two streamers at once.

- Encourage individual children to perform their own ribbon dance for the group.

Build a Giant Sensory Tube

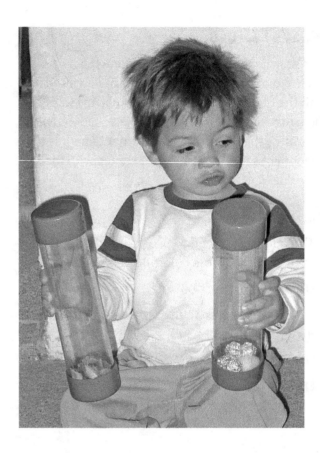

We found that clear plastic storage tubes, meant for storing nails, string, and other small items, make great sensory tubes for infants and toddlers. Children will enjoy observing the reaction of the tube's contents while they shake, rattle, and roll them around. They are easy to build, fun, and pretty durable.

Ages
12 mos.
and up

Materials

☐ Clear storage tubes

☐ Superglue

☐ Sensory items for tubes

Tools

None

Estimated Build Cost

The storage tubes cost between $2 and $5 depending on size.

Directions

1. These storage containers consist of a clear plastic tube with colored plastic end-caps. One end cap is usually already permanently attached and the other may have a slot cut in it for easy retrieval of stored items. If one end is not already adhered to the tube, the first step is to attach it with a few drops of superglue.

2. Now we need to seal the slot in the other end cap, if it has one (they usually do). Put a piece of duct tape on the inside of the cap to seal the slot and then apply a few drops of superglue to the other side of the slot and hold it closed until the glue sets.

3. The hard part comes next: you have to decide what to put into your tube. The possibilities are almost endless. We made three tubes as demos; one contained tinfoil and cotton balls,

> **TIP:** These tubes stand up to use by infants and toddlers, but we have lost a few due to schoolagers. It seems that older kids want to stand on the tubes. We suggest you make sure you train your older children well or keep them away from the tubes.

one contained small bits of colored construction paper, and the other was filled with small packing peanuts. Choose items that are readily available. You can test different options before sealing the other end onto the tube. Try a variety of objects to make sure they have visual and auditory interest. Do not use any liquid in your tubes. They will not hold water; all you'll get is a big mess. Find things that look and sound nice. We suggest that you avoid items that will make too much noise and drive you crazy.

4. When you're happy with the items, just secure the other end of the tube with a few drops of superglue.

Storage

You can store a number of these tubes in a small tote when not in use.

What's Learned

Children's eyes and ears will be stimulated when they see and hear the items in the tubes move. They will also learn about cause and effect relationships; their movement makes the items in the tube move. Shaking and rolling the tubes is also a great way to promote small- and large-muscle development in small children.

Variations

- Select items with a variety of colors so you can discuss their names with the children as you play.

- Make the tubes available to older children during dramatic play; experienced players will find all kinds of ways to integrate the tubes into their play.

- Involve older children in selecting the items to put in the tubes. They will love making items for the younger kids, and it's a great outlet for their budding imaginations.

Jump Ropes

We have worked in programs that have included both children and jump ropes for going on twenty years and have found very few jump ropes that will hold up to the use and abuse they receive. Now we know a simple length of rope will make a serviceable and long-lasting jump rope, but we want something with handles, something that looks like a jump rope. The wooden handles crack or splinter after hitting the ground a few times and the plastic ones are usually flimsy or poorly attached. The jump rope described below will stand up very well to lots of jumping and use as a dramatic play prop.

Ages
3
and up

Materials

☐ ⅜-inch rope

☐ Two 4-inch sections of ½-inch Schedule 40 PVC

☐ Two ½-inch Schedule 40 PVC end caps

☐ Three ½-inch Schedule 40 PVC pipe connectors

Tools

☐ Scissors

☐ Cordless drill with ⅜-inch bit

☐ Pliers

☐ Masking tape

☐ Hot-glue gun

Estimated Build Cost

$15 should buy enough rope (100 feet) and pipe to make fifteen 6-foot jump ropes. If you grab the pipe from your Pipe Construction Set, you can get by with only spending a few dollars on rope.

Directions

1. We'll do the hard part first. Drill a ⅜-inch hole through each PVC end cap. Use the pliers to grip the caps firmly as you drill. Do not try to hold the end cap with your hand. The piece will try to spin and you will risk an injury. If you are uncomfortable with this step, ask someone with more power tool experience to do it for you.

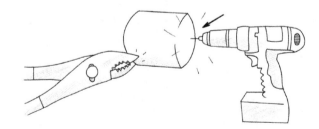

> **TIP:** Make sure children using jump ropes are always well supervised and know not to place the rope around their necks. Play safe.

2. After your holes are drilled you will need to determine how long to make your jump ropes. This will depend on the size of the children who will use them. You may also want to make a longer rope for use by a group.

3. Add about 12 inches to your desired final length. Wrap some tape tightly around where you plan to cut the rope. This will help you get a clean cut and keep the rope from fraying.

4. After making the cut, thread the three PVC pipe connectors onto the rope. These pieces will self-center on the rope when it is spun, and their added weight will draw the rope to the ground for easier jumping.

5. Now add an end cap onto each end of the rope; make sure you have about 12 inches of rope pulled through the cap on each end. Then push the rope's outer casing down and cut out about 6 inches of the rope's core.

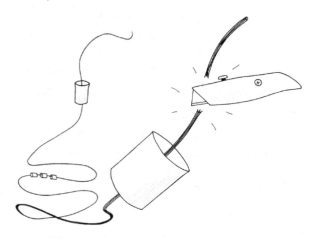

6. The next step is to knot the outer casing a few times so that it will not pull back through the hole.

Cut off any excess rope casing after the knot. Do this on both sides and then pull the caps so they meet their corresponding knots.

7. The last step is to hot-glue a 4-inch pipe section into each end cap. You can use PVC cement instead of hot glue if you have it available. You've just created a very durable kid-size jump rope. Have fun.

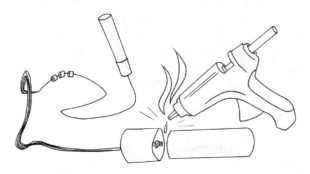

Storage

Store your jump ropes with your other outside play equipment.

What's Learned

Jump ropes are great for developing large-muscle skills and coordination. They will also come in handy as props for all kinds of active dramatic play.

Variations

- Vary the length of the ropes you make to meet the needs of different children.

- Play with your jump ropes inside and out.

- Jump ropes make great fire hoses, rescue lines, and other props during dramatic play.

Hinge and Latch Board

Materials

☐ 12-by-24-inch piece of ¾-inch thick wood

☐ Assorted hinges, latches, and hooks

Tools

☐ Cordless drill with ⅛-inch and ¹⁄₁₆-inch bits

☐ Phillips and flat-head screwdrivers

☐ Pencil

☐ Sandpaper, 100-120 grit

☐ Rag

Estimated Build Cost

This project should cost you between $15 and $25 to build.

Directions

1. Use your sandpaper to make sure the board is smooth and take the time to gently round the edges and corners to prevent splintering. The hardware you select should be small to medium in size; don't select a huge set of hinges or a giant gate latch. Keep the size of your board in mind when shopping.

2. Next, lay out your assorted hardware to ensure that it all fits and that there is room for its operation. Leave plenty of open space between items. If things are too crowded, children can get confused. You do not want to crowd too many items onto the board.

3. After you are happy with the layout, mark the hole locations with your pencil.

4. The next step is to drill pilot holes for all the screws. This will reduce the risk of splitting your board and make driving the screws easier. The ¹⁄₁₆-inch bit should do the job in most cases, although the larger ⅛-bit might be necessary.

This project will last nearly forever and it will entertain young children for almost as long. It's simple: a piece of wood with a variety of hinges, latches, and hooks that they can manipulate. They will love playing with all the moving parts.

Ages
18 mos.
and up

Defer to the instructions that come with the hardware when it comes to pilot-hole size.

5. After drilling all your holes, install the hardware with your screwdrivers. You could use the drill to do this, but the small screws are easy to strip and hard to hold onto while using a power tool.

6. After all the pieces are attached, wipe the whole thing down with a rag to remove any debris; many pieces will be covered with a light coat of oil.

7. This project is easy to use; just put it in front of the kids and step out of the way. They will instinctively start manipulating the hardware. We introduced this activity board to many children and not once were we asked, "How do you use this?"

Storage

This item will fit nicely on a shelf or in a large tote.

What's Learned

This project is great for developing small-motor skills in young children. It also teaches about cause-and-effect relationships while allowing tactile exploration of the materials.

Variations

- Mount the board directly to a wall at child height.
- Ask older children to practice manipulating the objects with their nondominant hand or even their toes.

Domino Block Set

Have you ever stood dominos on end so you could topple them? What fun. So much fun that we had to design some blocks that were easier for little fingers to maneuver. The children in our program soon discovered all sorts of other uses for these blocks as well. One sheet of plywood will make 1,024 of these versatile and fun blocks. The children will enjoy each and every one of them.

Ages
12 mos.
and up

Materials

☐ 4-by-8-foot sheet of ½- or ⅝-inch cabinet-grade plywood

☐ Sandpaper, 100–120 grit

Tools

☐ Table saw

☐ Electric miter saw

☐ Someone comfortable using the above machines

Estimated Build Cost

A good sheet of plywood will cost between $45 and $75. Don't try to save money here; make sure you buy good materials or you will end up with poor quality and possibly an unsafe product. We suggest that you share the cost of materials with other early childhood educators and split the resulting blocks. You can also purchase a half sheet of plywood for about three-quarters of the cost.

Directions

1. We strongly recommend that you find someone who has a table saw he or she is very comfortable using to cut these blocks for you. This is not a hard project if you have the right tool and know how to use it properly. It is, however, very dangerous if you do not know what you are doing. We have shared these blocks with many care providers at conferences, and there have been very few who did not have a friend, neighbor, or family member who would be ready and willing to safely cut blocks for them. Look around and find the help you need.

2. When you, or your volunteer, are ready, the cutting can begin. We want to cut the 4-by-8-foot sheet of plywood into 1,024 pieces that are each 1⅜ by 2⅞ inches. With a sharp blade, rip the plywood into thirty-two 1⅜-inch strips. Lightly sand the sides of these strips to remove any burrs or splinters.

3. These strips should then be crosscut with the miter saw into the 2⅞-inch lengths. They will need some light sanding, but not much if the saw blades are sharp.

4. This is a lot of blocks. Another good idea is to use them as gifts. A set of these blocks makes a wonderful birthday or holiday gift for young children, especially if they have played with them in your program.

5. To use, simply make a row of upended blocks spaced an inch or two apart and topple it. The kids will quickly start building and toppling on their own.

Storage

Plastic milk crates are great for storing these blocks.

What's Learned

These blocks are great for working small-muscle skills and learning about cause-and-effect relationships, hand-eye coordination, and engineering. The children will also find all kinds of ways to integrate these blocks into their dramatic play. Other learning will take place with the variations below.

Variations

- Build stuff with them; they're blocks!
- Grab a marker and add faces to a few blocks to create people.
- Let the children decorate some of the blocks with markers.
- Add them to the dramatic play area, where they will become money, food, and other necessary items in the worlds the kids create.

Working at the Car Wash

This is another great summer fun idea. Hooked up to the garden hose, this project becomes a drive-through car wash for all riding toys and imaginary vehicles. Kids will love to put on their swimsuits and take turns driving or walking under the falling water.

Ages
12 mos.
and up

Materials

☐ Garden hose

☐ Two 10-foot sections of 1½-inch Schedule 40 PVC pipe

☐ Two 1½-inch Schedule 40 PVC 90-degree elbows

☐ Two 1½-inch Schedule 40 PVC wye-fittings

☐ Three 1½-inch Schedule 40 PVC caps

☐ 1½-inch pipe connector

☐ 1½-inch bushing with ¾-inch pipe threads

☐ ¾-inch brass female hose adapter

Tools

☐ Cordless drill with a ⅛-inch bit

Estimated Build Cost

It will cost less than $15 to build this project.

Directions

1. Cut two 4-foot sections from the first section of pipe.

2. From the second pipe cut a 5-foot section and four 12-inch sections.

3. To build your car wash, select the two wye-fittings and insert a 12-inch pipe into the two parallel holes; these will serve as the project's feet.

4. Add a pipe cap to the ends of three of the feet.

5. Now insert a 4-foot piece of pipe into the remaining hole of each wye-fitting.

6. Attach a 90-degree elbow to the other end of each 4-foot section.

7. Next connect the two leg sections with the 5-foot pipe. What you have built should look like a large version of the hurdle from chapter 8.

8. The next step is to make the connections needed to hook the unit up to the hose. Insert the bushing into the pipe connector and then screw the brass hose adapter into the bushing.

9. All you have to do now is connect this section to the foot without a cap. This is where you will attach your garden hose when you're ready to play.

10. You should use PVC cement to permanently attach the feet to the upright pieces and the 90-degree elbows to the cross piece. This will allow you to break the unit down for storage and give it the strength it needs to stand up to heavy use.

11. Now use your drill to make a series of ⅛-inch holes along the underside of the 5-foot cross section. Start with about eight evenly spaced holes.

12. Attach the hose and see how it works. If the water seems to be exiting the holes under too much pressure, turn down the water or add a few more holes.

13. To play, introduce children to the car wash and supervise the fun. We promise you will not need to explain how to use this piece of equipment.

Storage

In the off season, store this project in a corner of the garage. It can also be stored under a deck or left outside since it is completely weatherproof.

What's Learned

Children will learn the same things they learned with the last water play project: cause-and-effect relationships, fluid dynamics (how water acts), and logical thinking, along with the motor skills and social skills that come with such activities. This is a wonderful sensory activity as well. They will also learn that cool water feels wonderful on their hot skin during a sunny afternoon.

Variations

- Introduce play money or car wash tokens so drivers can "pay" for their car wash.

- Add some buckets, rags, and sponges for more water fun.

- Squirt a bit of dish soap into the structure before connecting the hose to add some suds to the fun.

- Holes can be placed along the top or sides of the horizontal pipe for a different effect.

- Have children plug holes with their fingers and see what happens.

- Add a hole or two to the 4-foot uprights so the water comes out horizontally as well as vertically.

- Use the faucet to vary the water pressure. You can make it drip or spray from the holes depending on the faucet setting.

Magnet Bag Manipulatives

This project gives young children hands–on experience with magnets without the risk of pinched fingers. Playing with this set of eight magnet bags is a wonderful way to let children explore magnetism.

Ages **12 mos.** and up

Materials

- ☐ Four ceramic magnets, about ⅜ by ⅞ by 1⅞ inches
- ☐ Steel washers, box of 100
- ☐ Rice
- ☐ Fabric, cotton or cotton blend
- ☐ Thread

Tools

- ☐ Scissors
- ☐ Funnel
- ☐ Sewing machine
- ☐ Needle

Estimated Build Cost

The materials for this project should cost between $10 and $15.

Directions

1. Cut eight pieces of fabric 4 inches wide and 8 inches long.

2. Fold the eight pieces in half, finish-side in.

3. Sew two open sides of each square shut leaving a ½-inch margin.

4. Reverse the fabric so the finish side is now facing out.

5. Place a magnet in each of the first four bags and twenty-five washers in each of the other four.

6. Use a funnel to add rice to each of the bags. Fill them, but make sure you allow the room you will need to sew the final side shut.

7. Turn the fabric edges in and hand-stitch the final side of each bag shut.

8. Work the bags with your hands to center the magnets and washers.

9. The children will love exploring these manipulatives because some "stick" together, while some do not, and sometimes the bags will jump when another bag is moved near them in just the right way. To play, make the bags available and the children will do the rest.

Storage

Store your magnet bags in a large freezer bag.

What's Learned

First and foremost, the magnet bags teach about magnetism. Some bags will be attracted to each other, some will not. Some bags will repel others, some will not. Children will take note of these relationships while they play. At the same time they will be learning about cause-and-effect relationships. They will soon discover that if they put certain bags close together, the effect will be attraction. This is a great way to pique a child's curiosity and desire to discover and learn. Their senses will become engaged when they see some bags move toward or away from others on their own, and they will feel the tug of the magnets as they try to separate two attached bags.

Variations

- Test other items to see if they will stick to the magnet bags.

- See if children can make all eight bags stick together at the same time.

- Consider using one color of fabric for the bags with magnets and another color for the bags with washers.

Peg Board Geo Board

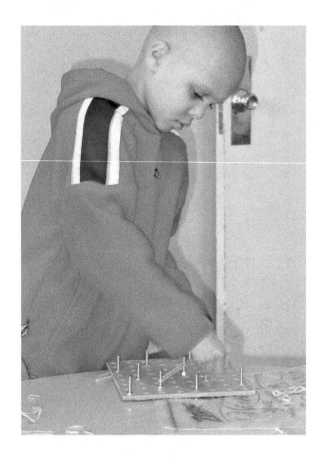

You can turn a few lacing boards from the Stitching Their Way into Literacy activity in chapter 7 into geo boards, with some hardware and a little bit of time. Geo is short for geometric. This activity will introduce children to a host of new terms and concepts, but they will probably be too busy exploring and discovering to notice they are learning.

Ages
18 mos.
and up

Materials

☐ Four 8-by-8-inch squares of peg board (these were made in chapter 7)

☐ 1¼-inch size-10 pan-head machine screws

☐ Nuts to match the above screws

☐ Rubber bands, assorted sizes and colors

Tools

☐ Screwdriver

☐ Pliers

Estimated Build Cost

Enough peg board to make four geo boards will cost around $6. A box of 100 screws and one with 100 nuts should cost around $8 total. A bag of assorted rubber bands will cost a few dollars. We have seen early childhood catalogs that charge around $40 for a set of five boards.

Directions

1. See the Stitching Their Way into Literacy instructions on pages 74–75 if you need directions for cutting the peg board sections.

2. Once you have your four sections of peg board, all you need to do is insert screws into some of the holes, from the bottom up, and hand-tighten a nut from the top side.

TIP: Supervise younger children well since the rubber bands are a choking hazard.

TIP: Make sure you do a thorough job picking up the rubber bands so they don't fall into the wrong hands or mouths.

3. You can place the screws in a pattern or install them completely at random. We recommend you do each board differently to add more variety to the activity.

4. Once you are satisfied with the layout of the screws, you can tighten them a bit with the pliers and screwdriver. Don't make them too tight— just enough to firm them in place.

5. Now just demonstrate to the children how rubber bands can be stretched over, around, and between the screw shafts to form shapes and patterns. They will be ready and willing to explore and discover on their own with little assistance.

Storage

Store your rubber bands in a plastic freezer bag and stick them on a shelf with the boards. Stack the boards face-to-face so they will take up less space.

What's Learned

This activity helps children discover shapes, angles, lines, patterns, and other geometric and mathematical concepts. Children will also work their small-muscle skills and learn to see negative space. These are valuable pre-reading and pre-writing skills. Creativity is also a big part of this activity. Children will love putting their imaginations to work creating shapes with the rubber bands.

Variations

- Periodically rearrange the screw patterns on your boards to keep them fresh.

- Allow older children to arrange the screws on the boards. This is a good small-muscle activity that will let them be in charge of something. Help with the final nut tightening if needed.

- Use nylon twine or pipe cleaners instead of rubber bands.

- Make two matching boards and let children create a pattern on one board and challenge a peer to re-create it on the other board.

- Use their interest in the geo boards to introduce new vocabulary. This is a great time to help children increase their grasp of mathematical terminology.

Peg Board Construction Set

Combine a variety of peg board pieces with some hardware and you have a durable and engaging building set that will empower children to create.

Ages
3
and up

Materials

☐ Peg board

☐ ¾-to-1¼-inch long size-10 pan-head machine screws and nuts

☐ ¾-inch angle or "L" brackets

Tools

☐ Table saw and an experienced operator

☐ Power miter saw and an experienced operator

Estimated Build Cost

The machine screws and nuts will cost around $5, and a partial sheet of peg board will cost less than $10.

Directions

1. The big part of the preparation process for this project involves cutting the peg board pieces to size. We are not going to tell you exactly what size to make your pieces or how many to make; you can determine that with the help of the person running the saw if you're not doing it yourself. We will give you some guidelines based on our experience:

- You want to create pieces of a variety of lengths and widths.

- Make sure you have multiples of each size.

- To avoid breaking, do not make pieces that are one-hole wide or any longer than six holes in length.

- Do not make any pieces bigger than 9-by-9-holes square.

2. After these pieces are cut, it's time to play. The different screw lengths allow children to connect different numbers of peg board layers, and the angle brackets allow them to connect pieces at right angles.

3. Some children may need help starting the nuts on the screws. They may get frustrated easily if unsuccessful. We found that simply being nearby to help with the first few twists is usually all the help they need. Most children catch on to the process quickly.

Storage

Store the screws and nuts in a small plastic bag and then store that bag and the peg board pieces in a large freezer bag.

What's Learned

Children can let their imaginations run wild while building with this construction set; this play set is a great way to encourage creative thinking. This activity is very empowering because it puts children in control of the process of creation. They are in control of what they build and how it is built. Children will also develop their hand-eye coordination and small-muscle skills while manipulating the screws and nuts.

Variations

- Add some cable ties or lacing strings to the mix for more creativity.

- Challenge children to build specific things: a cube, the letter M, or a stick figure.

- Provide a screwdriver, pliers, and a tape measure so they can build with real tools.

Hardboard Building Set

Hardboard is manufactured from wood fiber and is usually used for things like bookcase or cabinet backs. It is kind of like peg board without the holes. We have found that sections of hardboard are a great addition to any block collection. Among other things, the flat sections make great roofs, floors, roads, and fences. Children will find all kinds of uses for this versatile material.

Ages
12 mos.
and up

Materials

☐ Tempered hardboard, ¼ inch thick

Tools

☐ Table saw and an experienced operator

☐ Power miter saw and an experienced operator

Estimated Build Cost

A 4-by-8-foot sheet of tempered hardboard will cost around $12 and make more blocks than you'll need. Consider splitting the costs with other providers or purchasing half or quarter sheets of the material.

Directions

1. All you have to do is have someone comfortable using a table saw and power miter saw cut your sheet of tempered hardboard into smaller sections. We recommend about 4 inches wide and about 12 inches long. You can vary the width, but pieces any longer than 12 inches will have a tendency to bend and snap. We made ours all the same size for simplicity. You may choose to make different sizes.

2. To play, just put the new blocks in your play area. Within fifteen minutes of discovering the blocks at our house, RJ, who is three years old, informed us that he needed more pieces. He had created an intricate system of roads with the thirty or so blocks we made, but he still had building to complete. Children will be very eager to test out these new materials and figure out how they can be used with existing play items. We cut more pieces ASAP!

TIP: Hardboard is not waterproof. Make sure you keep your hardboard and peg board projects dry. Too much moisture will cause them to warp and start to fall apart.

Storage

These blocks will get used a lot. Store them with your other blocks so they are easily accessible when it is block play time.

What's Learned

These blocks will encourage creative and imaginative play. They will expand the way children use other blocks and dramatic play props. If they use them as ramps or in towers, they will learn about gravity; if they use them as serving trays in a game of restaurant, they will learn social skills. The versatility of these props is their chief charm.

Variations

- Make the hardboard blocks available during dramatic play.

- Use them to make giant letters and numbers on the floor.

- Lay the blocks out in a pattern on the floor and let the children take turns walking on them. This is a great large-motor activity.

- Standing on edge, they make great fences for plastic cows, horses, and dinosaurs.

Black-Light Box

Children of all ages will love seeing toys, markers, and other items glow when placed in the black-light box. This project is a way to put a new spin on old activities. We were amazed to see how many everyday items in our program began glowing when we started testing things under the light.

Materials

- ☐ Large dark-colored storage tote and lid; we used a 14-gallon 24-by-16-by-12.5-inch tote
- ☐ 18-inch fluorescent light fixture and bulb
- ☐ Machine screws and nuts to mount the fixture to the tote

Tools

- ☐ Cordless drill with ¼-inch bit
- ☐ Screwdriver
- ☐ Pliers
- ☐ Utility knife

Estimated Build Cost

The tote, fixture, bulb, and nuts will cost you around $30.

Directions

1. This is a fairly easy project to build. Start by cutting a small hole near one corner of the tote's bottom. You want to make a hole large enough to thread the light fixture's plug through. A 1-by-1-inch hole should do the job.

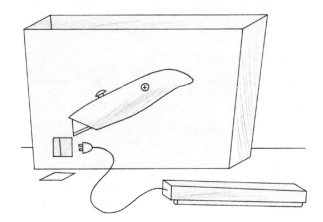

2. The next step is to mount the fixture on the long side nearest the hole you just cut. We cannot give detailed instructions for this step because there are so many types of totes and fixtures available. We can, however, provide the following tips we learned from building our prototype:

- Mount the fixture deep enough into the box so that you can still snap the lid in place.
- Position the fixture so that most of the light is cast into the box, not toward the opening.
- Use screws long enough to compensate for any contours in the tote's surface.

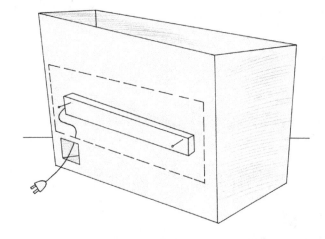

3. Now turn the tote on its side with the long side opposite the light fixture as the bottom and then install the bulb, thread the cord through the hole, and plug in the fixture. A purplish light should now bathe the inside of the tote.

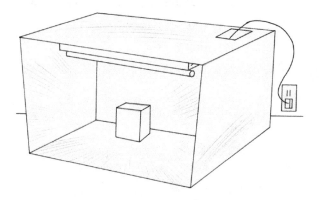

4. The first thing we did when we got to this point was eagerly try items that we thought would glow. We will describe some of the things we discovered in the Variations section.

5. Because of the tote's size, this project works best when used by one child at a time. Even two children have a hard time seeing and touching everything; more than two is a mess. This is a great chance to practice taking turns. Make a list of names and let the children help check their names off when it is their turn. This will show them how useful writing can be in everyday life.

6. Like so many other activities in this book, time is the key to successful play. Make sure each child receives the time needed to fully explore and play. If this means it takes a few days for everyone to get his or her turn, so be it.

Storage

When not in use, the tote can be used to store all your fluorescent manipulatives and art supplies. Store these items in freezer bags and keep the bags in the tote.

What's Learned

The black-light box provides a new environment in which children can experience a variety of activities. This has a tendency to make mundane activities new and fresh. Playdough is fun, but fluorescent playdough under the black light is a novel experience. Children will learn depending on the activity they do in the black-light environment. See the Variations list for other possible activities.

Variations

- Encourage children to test new items under the black light. Have them hypothesize whether the items will glow when placed under the light and then test their hypotheses.

- Write with fluorescent markers or highlighters.

- Use fluorescent paint.

- Cut fluorescent paper.

- Bend and twist fluorescent pipe cleaners.

- Manipulate fluorescent playdough.

- String fluorescent beads.

- Mix a small amount of fluorescent paint with water in a clear plastic bottle to create glow-in-the-dark sensory bottles. Add other fluorescent and nonfluorescent doodads to the water.

- Start a collection of fluorescent manipulatives. If it looks fluorescent it probably is fluorescent. One-year-olds will love to sit on your lap and play with the glowing items.

- Use the black-light box to display the projects children create with the fluorescent craft supplies. Parents will love to see their children's glowing works of art.

- Read books. We have found that many popular children's books look wonderful under the black light.

Light Box

The early learning catalogs sell light tables for $200 to nearly $500. We are going to show you how to build one for much less money that is easy to store and just as educational and entertaining as the expensive versions. The children in your program will love seeing the light shine through all kinds of translucent materials placed on the light surface. Build and enjoy this project.

Ages
12 mos.
and up

Materials

☐ Shallow transparent plastic tote, about 23 by 16 ½ by 6 inches

☐ Two 18-inch fluorescent light fixtures

☐ White paint appropriate for finishing plastic; we recommend using spray paint

☐ Two-sided mounting tape

☐ Duct tape

☐ Masking paper (old newspaper will work)

☐ Masking tape

Tools

☐ Utility knife

☐ Scissors

Estimated Build Cost

Expect to spend between $30 and $40 on this project. It is not cheap, but it is much less expensive than the store-bought versions and just as useful.

Directions

1. The first step is to cut a small notch about ½-inch wide and 1 inch deep in the lip of the tote that will allow the light-fixture cords to pass through.

2. The next step is to use mounting tape to secure the two light fixtures to the inside of the tote lid. The inverted lid will serve as the base of the light box. Make sure the fixtures are located so that the tote will still attach securely to the lid. It is best to position the lights, invert the tote, and test the fit before securing the lights. When you are happy with their location, fasten them with your mounting tape.

3. Now use your duct tape to fasten the two electrical cords together. Just wrap some tape around the cords every 6 to 12 inches. This will make them easier to manage and keep them from tangling. Make sure to leave the plug ends free so they can easily be inserted into an outlet.

4. Set this base unit aside and grab the tote.

5. What we want to do now is stop the light from shining out the sides of the tote and allow it to shine through the bottom. To do this, first cover the inside bottom of the tote using masking paper and tape.

6. In a very well-ventilated space, paint the inside of the tote. Follow the directions on the can and make sure you are using a paint that will stick to plastic. Use the wrong product and the finish will peel right off the tote. If you don't know what to use, ask the staff at your home center or hardware store.

7. You will probably want to give it two or three coats of primer to ensure a good finish. The paint does two things: it keeps light from going out the tote's sides, and it reflects that light out through our light box's play surface.

8. Allow the paint to dry and remove the masking paper.

9. Invert the tote and place it on the base unit. The previously masked area has become our light-table play surface.

10. Plug it in, turn on the lights, and test it out.

11. The size of the tote makes use of the light box impractical for more than two children at a time. This is a great time to practice taking turns. If possible, we recommend turning off the lights during light-box play, but we know that is not always practical. The Variations section below will give you some ideas on how to use the light box. Basically, anything you can do at a table that involves small manipulatives, writing, or crafts can be done at the light table. It adds a new dimension to these activities, and besides, it's fun.

Storage

To store this piece of equipment, just put the cord inside the tote and stick it on a shelf. You will also have room to store lots of translucent manipulatives or paper inside the tote.

What's Learned

Your light box will be useful for extending art and manipulative play so it will help children master all the skills and ideas that those learning areas encompass. Additionally, this project will help children learn about positive and negative space; they will be better able to see the objects they are manipulating (positive space) and the empty space around those items (negative space). This is an important part of learning to read and write because children have to learn to decode the text (positive space) on the page (negative space).

Variations

- Use playdough on the light box.
- Put together frameless puzzles on the light table.
- Write on the light box with translucent paper. Most white computer paper will work well, as will parchment paper.
- Start a collection of see-through manipulatives for the children to explore on the light table.
- Build with small blocks on the light table.
- The light table will add a new twist to any small manipulative or sorting activity.

Wire Nut Board

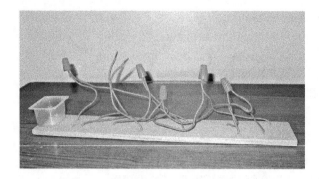

This activity board is a fun and unique small-muscle activity for children. It is fairly easy to build and very durable.

Ages
3
and up

Materials

☐ 12-gauge solid insulated copper wire, 6 to 10 feet

☐ Wooden base, oak (or other hard wood), approximately 4 by 24 inches and ½-inch thick

☐ Wire nuts

☐ Superglue

☐ Sandpaper, 100 grit

☐ Self-adhesive felt feet

Tools

☐ Wire cutter/stripper

☐ Cordless drill with ⅛-inch bit

Estimated Build Cost

You should be able to build this project for under $15.

Directions

1. Your first job is to drill ten to fifteen ⅛-inch holes through the surface of the board. The holes should be evenly spaced but random across the board's face.

2. Next lightly sand the board and gently round all corners and edges.

3. Cut a length of wire for each hole between 4 and 12 inches long.

4. The last ½ inch or so of one end of each wire should now be stripped to the copper. To do this, use the number 12 notch in your wire strippers. As you squeeze, the strippers will cut through the colored insulation but not the wire. You can then pull off and discard the insulation.

5. On the other end of each wire you want to remove only the last ½ inch of the clear plastic insulation that encases the colored insulation. To do this, use your wire stripper's number 10 notch. You will cut through and remove a very thin layer of clear plastic; this will allow the wire sections to fit perfectly into the holes you drilled.

6. Now apply a drop or two of glue to a wire and insert it into a hole so it is flush with the bottom of the base. Repeat until each hole has a wire.

7. Set the unit aside and let it dry for a day.

8. The last step of the construction is to place some felt feet on the bottom of the unit to keep it from scratching your tabletops or floors.

9. To use this unit, just line up two wires and twist on a wire nut. Bend and twist the wires into intricate shapes and see how far they will reach to find a mate. Younger children will be more successful removing the nuts and untwisting the wires. Older children will be able to put on and remove the nuts.

Storage

Fold the wires flat and the unit can be easily stored on a shelf or in a tote.

What's Learned

Manipulating the wires and twisting the wire nuts is a great workout for the small-muscle skills of young children. They will also feel great pride in their ability to take apart and put together the wires. The variations listed below offer more ideas to extend learning with this project.

Variations

- Use different-colored wire and nuts so you can discuss color with the children.
- Number each wire and challenge older children to add the numbers as they connect the wires.
- Have one child twist the wires and attach the nuts so another child can remove and untwist.
- Time children as they disconnect and untwist the wires.

Wire Bead Raceway

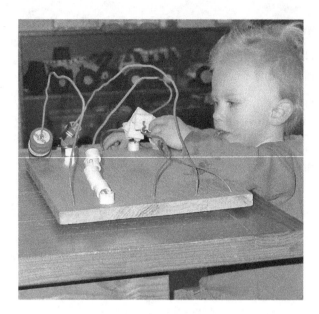

The catalog versions of this project cost $30 to over $50. Our version is not only less expensive, but also, we think, more versatile and easier to store, and it can be customized to fit your program. The children will enjoy guiding the beads along the different wire runs.

Ages
18 mos.
and under

Materials

☐ 12-gauge solid insulated copper wire, 10 to 16 feet

☐ Board, around 12 by 24 inches and ¾-inch thick

☐ Superglue

☐ Beads—we used items from the home center or recycling bin: PVC pipe, flexible electrical conduit, nuts, washers, sponges, and colored gallon-size-jug lids

☐ Felt feet

Tools

☐ Wire cutters

☐ Wire strippers

☐ Cordless drill with ⅛-inch bit

☐ Sandpaper, 100 grit

Estimated Build Cost

You should be able to construct this project for $20, give or take a few bucks. This is about half the catalog price for similar items.

Directions

1. The board you use for this project can be either solid wood or plywood. The first step of this project is to sand your board smooth and gently round all corners and edges.

2. Drill eight to twelve holes through the board's surface; make sure you choose an even number. Each of these holes will receive a wire end. Locate them randomly on the board's surface or drill them in a pattern that you choose.

3. Now cut half as many pieces of wire as you made holes (for example, twelve holes means six wires). Make sure each wire is long enough to reach between the holes you want it to connect, allowing plenty of extra wire for bends and curves between the holes.

4. To make your wire ends fit properly in the holes you drilled, use your wire cutters to strip off about ¾ of an inch of the thin coat of clear plastic that encases your wire. You can easily remove this plastic using the number 10 notch on your wire strippers. Remember, you only want to remove the thin clear coating, not the colored insulation.

5. Once you have removed the coating from both ends of each wire, you can begin test-fitting the wires. You can connect holes directly with a gentle arch, or you can use more wire and create loops and goofy paths for the beads to follow. The best part of this project is the wires' flexibility. You can reshape the paths of the wires whenever you choose.

6. After you arrange the wires in a way that you find satisfying, you can begin to add beads and glue them in place. Super-glue one end of a wire into its hole, add the beads of your choice to the wire, and glue the other end. Repeat for each wire.

7. The final step is to add some felt feet to the bottom of your project so it will not scratch your floors or tables. Set the unit aside so the glue can dry.

8. To use this project, all you have to do is set it in front of children. They will instinctively begin moving the beads along the wire paths.

Storage

Ease of storage is what makes this bead raceway better than the store-bought alternatives. Since we use flexible wire, you can flatten the wire runs before storing the unit and then fluff them up again when you want to use this activity again. The rigid wire of the store-bought versions means they take up a lot more space.

What's Learned

This piece of play equipment promotes small-muscle development and hand-eye coordination. This is also a great cognitive activity as children discover gravity and cause-and-effect relationships while pushing the beads along their tracks.

Variations

- Use a permanent marker to write letters or numbers on the beads to promote language and number awareness.

- Use beads of different colors so you can discuss them with the children as they play.

- Hang the board vertically for a different play experience.

INDEX OF ACTIVITY TITLES

INDEX OF ACTIVITIES BY AGE

While this index will be helpful in determining the age most children will find these activities engaging, you must also take into account the divine uniqueness of each child. Individual developmental levels vary over a wide spectrum; know the abilities and needs of each child.

Two Years and Up

Three Years and Up